UNIT 7 **HOW IRISH** **COMMUNICATE** **Page 35**	**Warm Up / Quotes Section** **Part 1A/B English/Irish & the World** *Origin of words* **Part 2A *As Gaeilge*** *Correct the sentences* **Part 2B Meaning from Context** *Choose answers* **Part 3 Interjections** *Listen & match* **Part 4A Gestures Quiz** *Test your cultural knowledge* **Part 4B Body Language** *Read & answer* **On Your Own**	***Main Discussion Areas*** *Features of Irish-English* *Colloquial language* *Gestures & body language* *Cultural communication* ***Follow-on Activities*** *Invent new words & language*
UNIT 8 **IRISH WEATHER** **Page 39**	**Warm Up / Quotes Section** **Part 1 Weather Vocabulary** *Categorise words* **Part 2A Describe Irish Weather** *Match expressions* **Part 2B Irish Invented Wind** *Read & match* **Part 3A Weather Quiz** *Answer questions* **Part 3B Discuss Irish Weather** *Read & answer* **Part 4 Become a Forecaster** *Make predictions* **On Your Own**	***Main Discussion Areas*** *Irish climate* *Weather signs in nature* *Weather & culture* ***Follow-on Activities*** *Make a video of your own* *weather forecast*
UNIT 9 **IRISH LEGENDS** **& LITERATURE** **Page 43**	**Warm Up / Quotes Section** **Part 1 Legend Characters** *Match pictures* **Part 2 Irish Heroes** *Reading comprehension* **Part 3 Labhraidh Loingseach** *Recreate the story* **Part 4 Irish Writers** *Read & match* **Part 5 First Lines** *Literary genres* **On Your Own**	***Main Discussion Areas*** *Typical legend characters* *Irish legends* *Irish writers* *First lines of books* ***Follow-on Activities*** *Write a short story / book review* *Invent your own legend*
UNIT 10 **IRISH SPORT** **& LEISURE** **Page 47**	**Warm Up / Quotes Section** **Part 1 Faster, Higher, Stronger** *Match symbols* **Part 2A Gaelic Games** *True or false / Explain rules* **Part 2B Irish Sporting Heroes** *Match pictures* **Part 3A/B/C Festivals** *Halloween, St. Patrick's Day etc.* **Part 4A/B Irish Drinks/Pubs** *Matching / Do's & Don'ts* **On Your Own**	***Main Discussion Areas*** *Olympic sports* *Gaelic games & Irish sportspeople* *Irish festivals* *Drink culture & Irish pubs* ***Follow-on Activities*** *Invent your own sports* *Watch or play an Irish sport* *Attend a festival in Ireland*
UNIT 11 **VISUAL IRELAND** **Page 51**	**Warm Up / Quotes Section** **Part 1 Irish Actors** *Match actor, role & film* **Part 2A/B Film Genres** *Match genres & descriptions* **Part 3A Your Image?** *Giving opinions* **Part 3B Irish Fashion** *Describing styles* **Part 3C Your Colour** *Personality quiz* **Part 4A/B/C City/Buildings/Home** *Match & discuss* **On Your Own**	***Main Discussion Areas*** *Good actors & types of films* *Irish fashion & image* *Architectural styles in Ireland* ***Follow-on Activities*** *Create your own film* *Design a fashion outfit* *Design a city/house*
UNIT 12 **IRISH SCIENCE** **& LOVE** **Page 55**	**Warm Up / Quotes Section** **Part 1A/1B World & Irish Inventions** *Match & order* **Part 2 Gulliver's Travels** *Survival game* **Part 3A/B I'd like…** *Write a poem. Rate characteristics* **Part 3C/D Romance Styles & Stages** *Matching* **Part 4A/B Love Languages** *Ordering & matching* **Part 5 Forbidden Love** *Read & reflect* **On Your Own**	***Main Discussion Areas*** *Inventions & inventiveness* *Science* *Romance, dating & relationships* ***Follow-on Activities*** *Create your own inventions* *Visit science museum* *Find out about romance in* *Ireland*

INTRODUCTION

THE IRISH CULTURE BOOK - STUDENT BOOK: ELEMENTARY/PRE-INTERMEDIATE includes a wide range of resources and activities designed to foster engagement and discussion on aspects of Irish culture. It can be used by any student with an interest in improving their English language skills and exploring areas of Irish culture.

THE IRISH CULTURE BOOK: ELEMENTARY/PRE-INTERMEDIATE is specifically aimed at those language students of below B1 level (A1/A2).

THE IRISH CULTURE BOOK is designed to give you, the student, opportunities to speak and think about topics that will be of interest about Ireland. The activities will help develop your conversation skills and improve your fluency through sharing ideas and observations. The conversations deepen critical thinking skills, helping to give the cultural awareness and speaking skills essential to be successful in a new culture and also for studying in college and university programs.

The material in THE IRISH CULTURE BOOK consists of twelve topic-based units on different areas of Irish culture, each filled with a variety of interesting and thought-provoking activities. The units all contain authentic texts. There are over three hundred and fifty questions, over one hundred quotations, including Irish proverbs and idioms; as well as questionnaires, matching and correcting exercises; reading, listening and vocabulary exercises; quizzes and creative problem-solving tasks. In many of the activities, students get to work together in pairs or small groups to reach a conclusion about a topic. A unique and important feature of the book is the inclusion of an 'On Your Own' section that calls on you to further investigate topics outside of the book, to initiate your own projects or to reflect on aspects of your own cultures in light of what has been discussed.

All the listening extracts used in THE IRISH CULTURE BOOK can be sourced online at **www.irishculturebook.com** and here can also be found further links and backup resources to each unit.

I hope you enjoy using this book.

IAN O'MALLEY

THE IRISH CULTURE BOOK 3

ELEMENTARY / PRE-INTERMEDIATE

STUDENT BOOK

by

IAN O'MALLEY

978-0-244-32494-0

Published by Malleyman Publications, Dublin, 2017.

TABLE OF CONTENTS

ALL LISTENING EXTRACTS CAN BE DOWNLOADED FOR FREE AT:
www.irishculturebook.com

MAP OF THE BOOK

UNIT 1 QUESTIONS ABOUT IRELAND Page 11	Warm Up / Quotes Section Part 1 Around the World *Match facts & countries* Part 2 Twenty Questions *Test your knowledge* On Your Own	***Main Discussion Areas*** *Facts about different countries* *Facts about Ireland* ***Follow-on Activities*** *Make your own 'country quiz'*
UNIT 2 IRISH FOOD Page 15	Warm Up / Quotes Section Part 1 Food Questionnaire *Work with a partner* Part 2 Famous Foods *Match foods & countries* Part 3 Hello Mr. Potato *Read & discuss* Part 4A Restaurants *Typical restaurant language* Part 4B Restaurant Menus *Create your own menu* Part 5 Irish Meals *Correct the mistakes* On Your Own	***Main Discussion Areas*** *Foods of different countries* *The potato in Irish culture* *Restaurant culture* *Meal times* ***Follow-on Activities*** *Create your own restaurant* *Share recipes*
UNIT 3 IRISH PHYSICAL CHARACTERISTICS Page 19	Warm Up Quotes Section Part 1 Passport Photographs *Find the nationality* Part 2 The Look of the Irish *Read & answer* Part 3 Facts about Red Hair *True or false quiz* Part 4A Appearance & You *Answer & discuss* Part 4B Attractiveness *Compare cultures* On Your Own	***Main Discussion Areas*** *Typical national appearance* *The Irish 'look'/Red hair* *Character and appearance* *Beauty in different cultures* ***Follow-on Activities*** *Make a true/false quiz* *Research national 'look' in your country & around the world*
UNIT 4 TRADITIONAL IRISH MUSIC Page 23	Warm Up / Quotes Section Part 1A Dance to the Music *Match pictures* Part 1B World Instruments *Listen & identify* Part 2A Traditional Irish Music *Read & answer* Part 2B Irish Instruments *Listen & identify* Part 3 Whiskey in the Jar *Analyse a song* Part 4 Irish Dancing *Read/answer. Watch & practice* Part 5 And Finally *Listen and imagine* On Your Own	***Main Discussion Areas*** *History of Irish music & dance* *Traditional instruments* ***Follow-on Activities*** *Invent a new instrument* *Investigate history of music in your country* *Learn Irish Dancing*
UNIT 5 MODERN IRISH MUSIC Page 27	Warm Up / Quotes Section Part 1 Find Someone Who *Class speaking activity* Part 2A Music Genres *Listen & match* Part 2B Describing Music *Music expressions* Part 3A Irish Singers *Identify singers/groups* Part 3B Irish Music Albums *Read for gist/Choose* Part 4 Irish Songs *Group decision-making/Listen* On Your Own	***Main Discussion Areas*** *Genres of music* *Talk about music* *Analyse song meanings* ***Follow-on Activities*** *Review an album* *Make a music video*
UNIT 6 A NICE CUPPA Page 31	Warm Up / Quotes Section Part 1A Famous Tea Drinkers *Match pictures* Part 1B A to Z of Tea *Find true & false sentences* Part 2A Ireland & Tea *Read & reflect* Part 2B Make a Pot of Tea *Word & sentence order* Part 3A Time for Tea *Cultural analysis & comparison* Part 3B 'No' to Tea in Ireland *Read & decide* Part 4 How <u>Not</u> to Make Tea *Spot the mistakes* On Your Own	***Main Discussion Areas*** *Tea & hospitality in Ireland* *Significance of small rituals* ***Follow-on Activities*** *Make your own A to Z list* *Investigate tea cultures* *Create an ad campaign*

NOTES FOR STUDENTS

The joy of conversation and discussion in a language – moments of exchanging ideas, sharing experiences, collecting information, laughter and more…

Welcome to THE IRISH CULTURE BOOK.

The topics in the book are designed so that hopefully they are relevant to your own experiences of, and interest in, Irish culture. The exercises and discussions will give you a better understanding of Ireland and its people. You will have lots of opportunities to think about many areas of Irish culture, and as a language learner, lots of possibilities for improving your language at the same time.

If you are using the book by yourself, feel free to use it how <u>you</u> want. You don't have to do each exercise in the order they appear in the book. If you think an exercise is too difficult for you or you are more interested in another topic, you can jump forward to something else. You can always come back to the original exercise later.

You don't need to answer or think about every question. Read the questions, and the quotations and select the ones that you are most interested in thinking about. Don't just think about them directly. Ask yourself - do the questions remind you of any experience you've had yourself in Irish culture or do they make you think about anything in your own culture?

*On THE IRISH CULTURE BOOK website, **www.irishculturebook.com,** you can find links to lots more resources for each unit as well as all the listening files for the book.*

Specific guideline notes for each unit, as well as a range of background information and answer keys, are available in THE IRISH CULTURE BOOK - Teacher's Resource Book.

And finally, the idea of the book is that we begin to think about and discuss, in English, what makes our cultures what they are. So don't be afraid to disagree with what you read in the book. Your ideas on Irish culture may be equally as valid as any of the observations offered in the book.

STRUCTURE OF A UNIT

Most units in the book follow the general structure outlined below.

WARM-UP Section

The questions in the WARM-UP section are intended as an initial introduction to the unit topic, focusing on the learner's personal experience and opinions, and also finding out how much, if anything, is known about the topic about to be discussed. For teachers, feel free to skip some or all of the questions or ask your own questions if you feel they are more appropriate for your particular class.

QUOTATIONS Section

The quotations present a wide range of ideas, viewpoints and perspectives. Quotations can be particularly appealing to language learners of all levels because they give an immediate, easy access into a piece of wisdom or life-view expressed in another language. Quotations are excellent for provoking debate and give the discussions a deeper perspective. There are many ways to use this section.

- For all users, feel free to read through all the quotations or focus on just a couple.
- Think about if there is any quotation you disagree with and why, or which quotation most reflects your own view.
- With proverbs, sayings or idioms, try to think if you have any similar or equivalent sayings in your own culture.
- As a teacher, you could ask students to read through the quotations themselves and to choose their favourite one and report back to the class.
- As a teacher of a multicultural class, you could ask students to translate any proverb, saying or idiom from their own language and share it with the class.

PARTS 1 - 5

Most units are divided into three to five parts. These parts are the main body of each unit and include quizzes, problem-solving activities, questions, short readings, listenings, matching exercises and more.

- For each unit, consult the instructions and supporting materials in the Supplementary Notes.
- It is not necessary to do every part of a unit depending on time constraints or interest or, for teachers, the language proficiency of your students
- Also, feel free to change the order in which you do these parts as you wish.

ON YOUR OWN Section

This section encourages you to think outside of the book or classroom. It may involve:

- Project or written work.
- Asking questions of Irish people about their ideas of the topic of the unit and reporting back.
- Reflection on the users' own cultures in comparison/contrast to Irish culture and reporting back.
- Further reflection on the users' own opinions and ideas on the topics raised in the unit.

ACKNOWLEDGEMENTS

I would like to thank all the people who supported and assisted in making this book possible.

Thank you to the talented and dedicated group of teachers who tested the materials with students and helped refine and improve many of the exercises - to Paula Barrett, Jane McGovern, David Kirwan and Helen Reilly in 'D6' and to Anthony Mannion, Shane O'Malley, Darragh, Robert, Daniel and Aisling in 'D2'. Thank you to these talented teachers and colleagues for their advice - to Niall, Ana, Aonghus, Felicity, Mark, Daniel and others.

Thank you to all the students of DCI who helped test and refine materials and provided a lot of fun while doing it.

A huge thank you to those who suggested amendments or came up with good ideas to include - to Shaun O'Malley, Jim Gorman, Eimear Gorman, Mark Rae, Dervla O'Malley, Vera O'Malley, Fiona McGinty, Nicoletta Giusti, Federico Black, Jimena Alvarez, Ruth Wall, Niamh Kelly and Ania Tomaszewska.

Thanks also to Jonathan McGlinn, aka Johnny Rayge, for permission to use his music in the book.

It has not always been possible to identify the sources of all the material used in the book and in such cases the publisher and author would welcome information from the copyright owners.

A special mention for two great teachers I've learned so much from - my uncle Tom and my aunt Ellen - and also for my friend Andrew who always inspired me to gaze further and think bigger.

Thanks and love to all my family who helped and supported at different points of the book - to all the O'Malleys, to Keelan and Evan and all the Finns, Leah, Cameron, Cian and all the Raes.

COMMENTS AND FEEDBACK
Your feedback is extremely welcome.
Please get in contact and let us know your opinions on the book.

E-mail:

ian@irishculturebook.com

Web-page:

www.irishculturebook.com

WARM UP

1. What do you know about Ireland?
2. Do you know any famous Irish people - actors, writers etc?
3. Do you think Ireland is very different from your country or similar?

PART 1 AROUND THE WORLD

Match each country with a fact and with a picture below.

A. Korea	B. Ireland	C. Argentina	D. Austria	E. Belgium
F. USA	G. Antarctica	H. Northern Ireland	I. Morocco	

FACT	COUNTRY	PICTURE
Two brothers invented the airplane in this country		
Tango dancing started here		
When you're born here, you're already one year old		
Schönbrunn Tiergarten - the oldest zoo in the world is here		
Fez the world's oldest university is here		
They built the Titanic here		
The government of the EU is here		
This country is the biggest exporter of bananas in the world		
Some people visit but nobody lives here		

1 **Brussels Sprouts**

2

3 **Claddagh Ring**

4 **Statue of Liberty**

5

6 **Sahara**

7 **Jedi Qui-Gon Jinn**

8

9 **Mozart**

Is your country here? What (other) facts and pictures would you use for your country?

QUOTES

Which is your favourite quote? Why?

"We have bad weather in Ireland, but the sun is in people's hearts."
– Marianne Williamson

"The great men of Ireland are all a little bit crazy. They fight and they are happy. They sing songs and they are sad."
– G.K. Chesterton

"Ireland is a place to start again and to change your life."
– Daniel Day-Lewis, Actor

"The moon and stars give you light that makes your heart feel better."
– Irish Saying

"'You're a different kind of Irish,' she said. 'Every Irish person is a different kind of Irish,' he said."
– Charles Brady

"Live a long life, for as long as you want. And never need anything for all of your life."
– Irish Saying

"The Irish have a lack of respect for everything and everybody. It's good."
– Brendan Behan, Writer

"Every man is friendly until a cow comes into his garden."
– Irish Saying

"Irish people – psychoanalysis doesn't work with them!"
– Sigmund Freud

What do you think about the quotes? Can you think of any similar quotes from your culture?

ÉIRE IRELAND

PART 2 TWENTY QUESTIONS ABOUT IRELAND
WHAT DO YOU KNOW ABOUT IRELAND? TEST YOUR KNOWLEDGE BELOW.

1. What symbol is on the front of all Irish euro coins?

2. What sea is to the east of Ireland? *A. Grey Sea B. Green Sea C. Irish Sea D. English Sea*

3. What is the Internet address for Ireland?

4. Name an Irish writer.

5. In what year did the South of Ireland get independence from England - 1882, 1922, 1962, 2002?

6. Can you give two examples of Irish surnames?

7. There are thirty-two counties in Ireland, (twenty-six in the South and six in the North). Name two.

8. What is the population of Ireland?

9. The festival of Halloween started in Ireland. On what date is it each year?

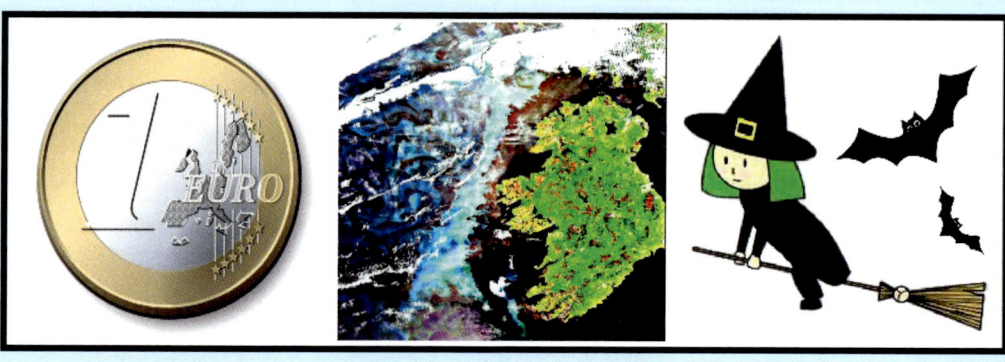

PART 2 TWENTY QUESTIONS ABOUT IRELAND *contd.*

10. Name one of Ireland's national sports.

11. Which of these was <u>not</u> invented in Ireland? *A. The submarine B. St. Patrick's Day parades C. Whiskey D. Colour Photography*

12. What is the international telephone code for Ireland (if you are calling from outside Ireland)?

13. Name an Irish singer or music group.

14. If you see 'KK' on a car registration number plate, what does it mean?

15. What is the most common eye colour in Ireland? **A.** Brown **B.** Green **C.** Blue

16. What colours are on the Republic of Ireland flag?

17. In 19th century Ireland millions of people died because of a problem with what vegetable?

18. Name one of Ireland's airline companies.

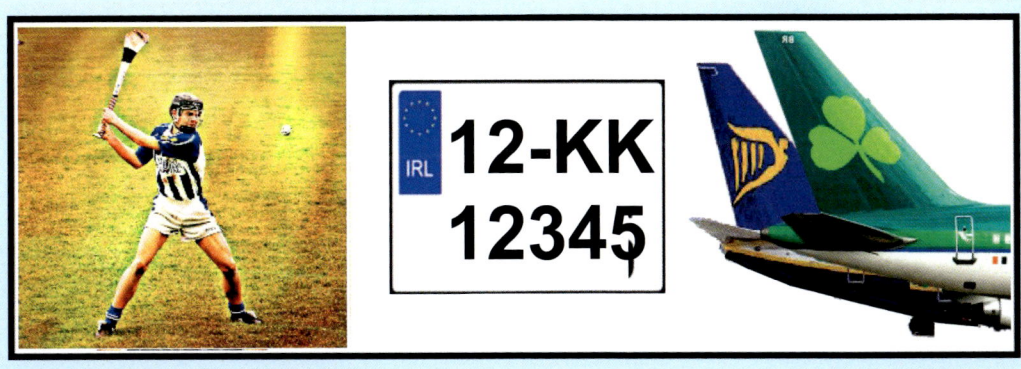

PART 2 TWENTY QUESTIONS ABOUT IRELAND *contd.*

19. What colour are post boxes in the Republic of Ireland? **A.** Red **B.** Green **C.** Yellow **D.** Blue

20. Is Ireland **A.** *the 10th* **B.** *the 20th* **C.** *the 30th* biggest island in the world?

BONUS QUESTION 1

Match the five Irish cities with their locations on the map of Ireland.

CITY	NUMBER ON MAP
Galway	
Cork	
Limerick	
Dublin	
Belfast	

BONUS QUESTION 2

Match the six pictures of Irish landmarks/monuments with their names and with the interesting facts about them.

1.   2.   3.

4.   5.   6.

NAME			
i.	Carlow Dolmen	iv.	The Causeway
ii.	Hill of Tara	v.	The Spire
iii.	Molly Malone	vi.	High Cross

INTERESTING FACT	
A.	Older than the Pyramids in Egypt
B.	There's also a famous song about her
C.	The old Kings of Ireland lived here
D.	There was once a bomb explosion on this spot
E.	The legend says that a magic giant built these
F.	A mix of Celtic & Christian culture

PICTURE	NAME	FACT
1		
2		
3		
4		
5		
6		

ON YOUR OWN

1. Look up more information about one question you found interesting.
2. Can you make some similar questions about your own country?

WARM UP

1. Name one food you like and one food you <u>don't</u> like.
2. Give an example of one food that is good for you and one food that is bad for you.
3. Do you know what a 'full Irish breakfast' is?
4. What is your favourite food that your mother or father cooks?

PART 1 FOOD QUESTIONNAIRE

Work in pairs. Fill in the questions below for yourself first and then ask your partner.

	YOU	YOUR PARTNER
Are you a good cook? Name one thing you can cook.		
What do you usually eat for breakfast? (Do you know what a traditional 'Irish breakfast' is?)		
Do you eat 'healthy' food? Name one good and one bad food that you eat.		
Do you like food from other countries? (Name one food you like from another country)		
What food would you <u>never</u> eat?		
What is a typical dinner in your country?		
Can you name one typical Irish food?		

Which is your favourite quote? Why?

"If you want to be friends with someone, go to his house and eat with him... the people who give you their food give you their heart." – Cesar Chavez

"Irish coffee has in one glass all the four important food groups: alcohol, caffeine, sugar and fat." – Alex Levine

"The most dangerous food is wedding cake." – James Thurber

"If someone really likes potatoes, they are always a good person." – A.A. Milne

"It is difficult to be leader of a country with 246 different types of cheese." – Charles de Gaulle, French Politician

"Healthy food is good for you but biscuits taste better." – Robert Redford, Actor

IRISH FOOD WISDOM

"A good mood starts in the kitchen."

"It's easy to give a friend half your potato when you love him or her."

"A small house with lots of good food is better than a big hungry house."

"Eating is the good part but paying for the food is the bad part."

"You laugh more when the food is good."

What do you think about the quotes? Can you think of any similar quotes from your culture?

'Doctor, don't tell me to eat better. I ate a salad once and I didn't feel any different.'

PART 2 FAMOUS FOODS

1. What food is your country most famous for?
2. Match the countries from the box below with the food each is famous for and with the pictures.

FOOD	COUNTRY	PICTURE
Hamburger		
Kebab		
Sushi		
Curry		
Feijoada		
Couscous		
Pizza		
Tacos		
Spring Rolls		

COUNTRY	A. Mexico B. Italy C. Turkey D. India E. USA F. Brazil G. China H. Japan I. Morocco

3. Which of the foods above would you most like to eat now? What food would you like to eat from your country right now?

PART 3 HELLO MR. POTATO

One of the most famous foods in Ireland is the potato! It has a long history, it's good for you and it tastes good.

Have you ever eaten Irish potatoes?

Answer the questions below.

1. Irish people eat more potatoes than anyone else in Europe – *true or false?*

2. Irish people were the first in Europe to eat potatoes – *true or false?*

3. In the 1840s, there was a big disaster in Ireland called the Great Famine. All the potatoes were bad. *How many Irish people died in this disaster? (Look it up online.)*

4. Many Irish people went to America after the Famine. *Find the names of two famous 'Irish Americans'?*

5. In 1995, the potato was the first vegetable to grow in a specific place. *Where?*

6. Potatoes are a healthy food. *What vitamins can you get from potatoes? (Look it up online.)*

7. Some Irish people like to eat potatoes everyday with their dinner. *What different things can you eat potatoes with? List 3 things. What different ways can you cook or prepare potatoes?*

Write down some information about the most famous food in your country.

UNIT 2 IRISH FOOD

PART 4A RESTAURANTS

1. Do you like going to restaurants? How often do you go to restaurants?
2. What is your favourite type of restaurant? Why?
3. **Match the typical questions in restaurants below with the answers on the right.**

1. 'Are you ready to order?' - **Waiter**	**A.** 'They're downstairs.' - **Waiter**
2. 'Can I have soup as a starter and steak for the main course?' - **Customer**	**B.** 'No, sorry. We only take cash.' - **Waiter**
3. 'How would you like your steak cooked?' - **Waiter**	**C.** 'Medium, please.' - **Customer**
4. 'Which wine do you think is the best?' - **Customer**	**D.** 'No, we need another few minutes to think, thank you.' - **Customer**
5. 'How is your food?' - **Waiter**	**E.** 'Yes. We'll have an Americano and a tea with milk.' - **Customers**
6. 'Excuse me, where are the toilets?' - **Customer**	**F.** 'No, thank you. We can't eat any more.' - **Customer**
7. 'Would you like to see the dessert menu?' - **Waiter**	**G.** 'This Italian red wine is very good.' - **Waiter**
8. 'Would you like a tea or coffee?' - **Waiter**	**H.** 'Of course. I'll get the bill for you now.' - **Waiter**
9. 'Can we have the bill, please?' - **Customer**	**I.** 'Very good choice.' - **Waiter**
10. 'Can I pay by credit card?' - **Customer**	**J.** 'It all tastes really good, thanks.' - **Customer**

1	2	3	4	5	6	7	8	9	10

PART 4B RESTAURANT MENUS

1. In pairs/small groups, make a menu for a typical restaurant from your country. Think of a name for your restaurant..
2. Can you also make a menu for a typical Irish restaurant?

Your Country – Restaurant Name	Ireland – Restaurant Name
Menu – Starter	Menu – Starter
Main Course	Main Course
Dessert	Dessert
Total Cost:	Total Cost:

'How would you like your alphabet soup madam? In CAPITAL LETTERS? In **BOLD?** *Italics?*'

3. Are Irish restaurants very different from restaurants in your country? For example, do you give a 'tip' (extra money) to the waiter? How much?
4. Which restaurant, the Irish one or the one from your country do you think would be better? Why?

PART 5 IRISH MEALS

1. *After your Irish breakfast...*

   In Ireland, the biggest meal of the day is dinner. Irish people usually eat dinner after they come home from work or study around 6 or 7pm. People eat lunch, normally a smaller meal than dinner, around the middle of the day. Supper is usually a small meal (a snack before going to bed).

   Look at the boxes below. Some of the foods are in the wrong places. Can you put each food in the correct box? Write the number of the box each food should be in.

   *Some foods are possible in more than one box.

1. BREAKFAST 8 - 9am		2. LUNCH 1 - 2pm		3. DINNER (& DESSERT) 6 - 7pm		4. SUPPER 9 - 11pm	
Potatoes		Bread		Ice Cream		Soup	
Orange juice		Ham & cheese Sandwich		Fish & Chips		Cup of tea	
Salad		Bowl of cereal		Chicken		Biscuits	
Apple tart		Chocolate cake		A banana		Irish stew	

2. What typical things do you eat in your country - for breakfast / for lunch / for dinner / for supper?
3. In your country, what time do you eat each meal at?

ON YOUR OWN

1. Stew has been Ireland's main national dish for over two hundred years. Have you ever eaten Irish Stew?

   Here is a recipe for Irish Stew.

TRADITIONAL IRISH STEW

INGREDIENTS	PROCEDURE
– 4 potatoes (sliced) – 4 onions (sliced) – 6 carrots (sliced) – 0.5 kg of bacon – 1.5 kg of lamb cut into small pieces – Salt and pepper – 2 ½ cups of water – 4 potatoes cut in half – Fresh parsley cut into small pieces	1. You will need a large pot for all the ingredients. 2. First put some sliced potatoes, onions, and carrots into the pot. 3. Now put in the bacon and lamb. 4. Put in some salt and pepper. 5. Repeat these three steps with more ingredients until you use all of the ingredients. 6. Add enough water to cover all the ingredients. 7. Put the potatoes (cut in half) on top of everything. 8. Cook the stew over a very low heat (Mark 1/2) for about 2 hours. 9. When the stew is cooked and ready to eat, put the parsley on top. 10. Serve in soup bowls. *Serves 4 to 6 people.*

2. Try cooking Irish Stew yourself.
3. Can you find any other typical Irish recipes? Eg. Irish soda bread or Dublin coddle etc.
4. Write a recipe for a typical food from your own country.
5. Cook some food and bring it in for the other students in your class to eat.

UNIT 3 IRISH PHYSICAL CHARACTERISTICS

WARM UP

1. Describe yourself. *Are you tall or short? What colour is your hair? What colour are your eyes? Etc.*
2. Describe a typical person from your country.
3. Compare a typical person from your country with an Irish person?

PART 1 PASSPORT PHOTOGRAPHS

1. The people in the photos below are famous. There are two actors, two singers, three sports stars, two political leaders and a painter. How many do you know? Can you match each with their nationality and what they are famous for? *(Look the names up online.)*

NATIONALITY	PICTURE	NAME/FAMOUS FOR
Spanish		
Italian		
Chinese		
Omani		
French		
Brazilian		
German		
Jamaican		
Columbian		
Irish		

2. How did you know which country each person comes from? What helped you? *(E.g. The Irish person has red hair and blue eyes.)*
3. Is there someone from your country here? If not, can you think of someone famous who looks like a 'typical' person from your country? Show a photo of them to your class.
4. Do you look like a 'typical' person from your country?

QUOTES

Which is your favourite quote? Why?

"Irish faces are intelligent – they have smiles on their mouths and sad eyes..."
– Henry Allen.

"After you are 30 years old, everyone is responsible for the face they have."
– Irish Saying

"'She looks Irish,' Halley said. 'She has white skin, blue eyes, red hair and she looks mysterious and romantic."
– Paul Murray.

"Everyone has beauty but not everyone can see it." – Confucius.

"Good manners and being polite are better than being good-looking or beautiful."
– Irish Saying.

"'You have the Irish look,' she said. 'What do you mean?' 'I mean that you're handsome. You are funny and you can enjoy life.'"
– Helen Birch

"Beautiful hair is the best answer to every problem." – Ivana Trump

"A face with no freckles is like a night without stars." – Irish Saying.

"And I ask you, friend, what is a fella to do? / Because her hair was black and her eyes were blue... I lost my heart to a Galway girl"
– Words from the song 'Galway Girl'

What do you think about the quotes? Can you think of any similar quotes from your culture?

PART 2 THE LOOK OF THE IRISH

Do you think the Irish person in PART 1, rugby player Paul O'Connell, looks Irish?
Can you think of any other 'typical' Irish person - a famous person or somebody that you know?

Read and answer the questions.

WHERE DOES THE IRISH LOOK COME FROM?

Many different groups of people have come to Ireland during its history. We don't know what the original people who arrived here 10,000 years ago looked like.

- What do you think the original Irish people 10,000 years ago looked like? Can you draw a picture of them?

The Celtic people arrived in Ireland about 500 BC. The Ancient Romans said the Celts were "very tall" and a lot of them had "red hair".

- In fact, most Celts had black hair. Why did the Romans think the Celts had red hair? What did the Celts do to their hair to make it look red?

- Most Celts were more or less the same size as the Romans. What did the Celts do to their hair that made them look really tall? (Look it up online.) What do you put in your hair?

Vikings began to attack Ireland in the 9th Century. They came to Ireland in ships from Scandinavia (Denmark, Norway and Sweden).

- What does a 'typical' Scandinavian person look like? Find some examples online.

The Vikings mixed with the Irish. Vikings married Irish Celtic people and they had families. The Vikings were blonde or red-haired with blue eyes.

- Can you see any 'Viking look' in Irish people now? Do many Irish have red or blonde hair and blue eyes?

Irish people today often have blue or green eyes and white skin with freckles.

- Do you have any freckles? Can you count them? Do you like freckles?

Irish people with white skin can have problems with the sun in the summer and they can get red (sunburnt) easily.

- Write down three pieces of advice you would give to an Irish person who is going to the beach on a sunny day in the summer?

White skin with dark hair is common in Ireland. The actor Colin Farrell (left) is a good example of this look. People think this 'look' comes from Irish women marrying Spanish sailors who came to Ireland in the 16th and 17th centuries.

- Are there different groups of people in your country who look very differently? Find some pictures online and show your class.

In ancient Celtic Ireland, hair colour was very important.

For example, Celtic people thought women and men with blonde or red hair were special and closer to God.

1. If you visit the National Archaeology Museum, Dublin, you will see the bog-body 'Clonycavan Man' (300 BC). You can still see his red hair.

2. In the Book of Kells (800 AD) in Trinity College, Dublin, you can see that Jesus usually has blonde hair and a red beard.

How did people look in your country in the past?

Is it different from now? *Find some pictures online.*

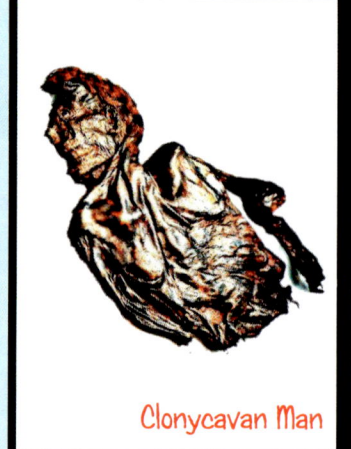

Clonycavan Man

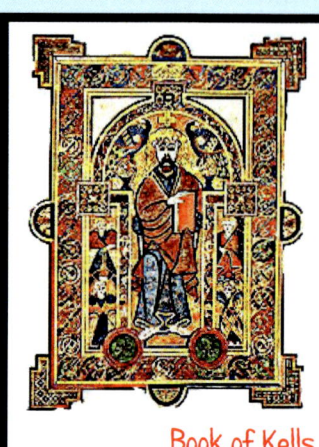

Book of Kells

UNIT 3 IRISH PHYSICAL CHARACTERISTICS

PART 3 TRUE OR FALSE - 10 FACTS ABOUT RED HAIR

Red hair is not very common in the world. Only about 2% of people in the world have red hair.
Red hair is quite common in Ireland. About **10%** of Irish people have red hair.

Which of the eight facts below about red hair are True or False?

RED HAIR FACTS	T/F
1. Red hair is easier to change colour, for example in the hairdressers, than other hair colours.	
2. Ancient Irish people thought 'redheads' (people with red hair) were magic. They touched a red-head's hair for good luck.	
3. People with red hair don't get grey hair.	
4. People with red hair more often write with their left hand than other hair colours.	
5. In about 100 years, there will be no more people with red hair in the world.	
6. Ancient Greeks thought people with red hair changed into vampires after they died.	
7. Red-haired people usually have more hairs on their heads than other colours.	
8. Red-haired people feel pain more than other colours.	

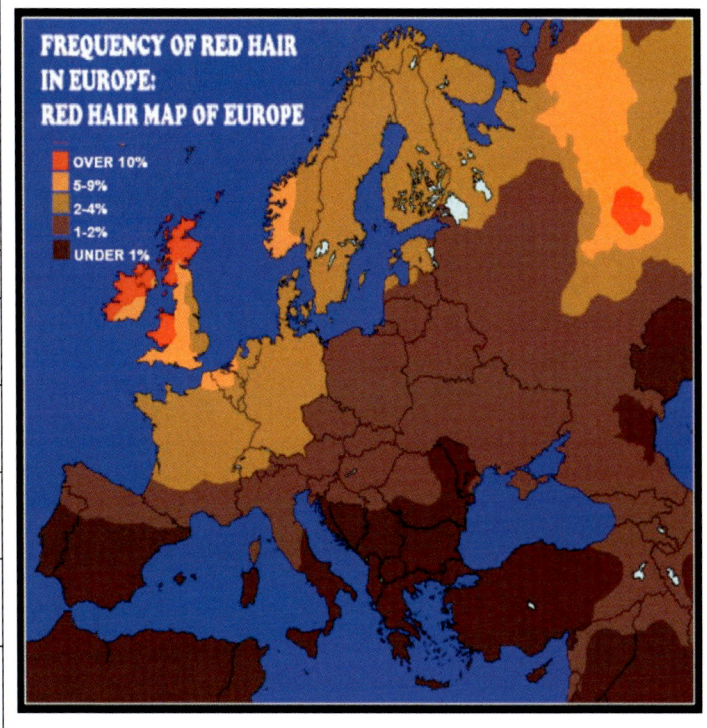

FREQUENCY OF RED HAIR
IN EUROPE:
RED HAIR MAP OF EUROPE

- OVER 10%
- 5-9%
- 2-4%
- 1-2%
- UNDER 1%

In pairs/small groups, can you make a list of True/False facts about one of the physical characteristics in the box below?
Ask the rest of your class if they think each of your facts is true or false.

Black / brown / blonde hair	Blue / green/ brown eyes	Losing your hair (being bald)
Being tall or short	Having big or small feet	Being a man vs Being a woman

PART 4A PHYSICAL APPEARANCE AND YOU

1. Think of a famous person you think is very attractive.

   Can you describe them? Write down reasons why you think they are attractive.

2. Beautiful vs. Handsome.

   Do you think men and women usually think different things are attractive?

3. When we see a beautiful person, we often think they are also friendly and happy.

   Do you think that beautiful people are generally happier than other people? Why?

4. "People with a 'baby' face – a round face and big eyes – are more honest."

   Is this true? Do you know anyone with a 'baby' face?

5. Beautiful people often get better jobs.

   Why? Is this fair?

6. "If you feel attractive, other people will probably think you are attractive too."

   Is this true? Write down three things that are attractive about you. (You can share them if you want!)

PART 4B CULTURE AND ATTRACTIVENESS

Answer the questions below. Work in pairs or small groups.

1. Is a beautiful person the same in Europe, Asia, Africa, America etc. or is 'beautiful' different in different cultures? Can you think of some examples of how it is different in different cultures?

2. Are the clothes in Ireland very different from your country? Can you give any examples of fashion in Ireland (or in your country) that you like and don't like?

3. In the past in Ireland, people thought fatter men and women were more attractive than slim people. Why do you think this was true? What body shape do people usually think is attractive now?

4. In Ireland in the past, a suntan (brown skin from the sun) was unattractive. Now people usually think a suntan is more attractive than white skin. Why do you think this has changed? Is this the same in your country?

NOW YOU

a. In which picture above do you think the woman looks most beautiful? Which country do you think each one is from?

b. In your country, what clothes would you wear to make yourself look beautiful or handsome for the two situations below? Write them down and compare with a partner.

   Situation A - *You are going to a disco on a Saturday night.*
   Situation B - *You are going for dinner in a good restaurant with your boyfriend/girlfriend.*

ON YOUR OWN

1. If you are in Ireland, look around you at the people. Can you describe the people you see? What different adjectives would you use to describe the people that you see? Use a dictionary to help you.

2. If you are in Dublin, visit the **Book of Kells** in Trinity College. Can you see the blonde-haired, red-bearded Jesus?

3. Visit the **National Museum of Archaelogy** and see the 'Clonycavan Man' with red hair and the other bog bodies.

4. **If Brad Pitt were Irish...**
   Think of somone famous. Imagine how differently they would look if they came from your country.

5. Listen to the popular Irish song 'Galway Girl' by **Sharon Shannon** and **Mundy**.
   The song is about a boy who falls in love with a pretty girl in Galway, who has dark hair and blue eyes.
   You can find a listening worksheet for the song in the *ONLINE RESOURCES SECTION.*
   www.irishculturebook.com/unit-3-irish-physical-characteristics/
   Can you fill in the gaps in the song?

6. Listen to the song 'Galway Girl' by Ed Sheeran. Which 'Galway Girl' song do you prefer?

UNIT 4 TRADITIONAL IRISH MUSIC

WARM UP

1. When do you like to listen to music - on the bus, when you're studying, lying in bed etc.?
2. Do you prefer listening to music from your own country or to international music? Why?
3. Can you play a musical instrument?

PART 1A DANCE TO THE MUSIC

a. Do you like to dance? Are you a good dancer?
b. Can you match the pictures with the famous dances below?

DANCE	PICTURE	DANCE	PICTURE
Breakdance *(USA)*		Disco *(USA)*	
Samba *(Brazil)*		Flamenco *(Spain)*	
Ballet *(Russia)*		Tango *(Argentina)*	
Haka *(New Zealand)*		Cossack *(Ukraine)*	
Bharatanatyam *(India)*		Gangnam *(South Korea)*	
Belly Dance *(Turkey)*		CanCan *(France)*	

c. Watch videos of each dance in the *ONLINE SECTION*.
What adjectives would you use to describe each dance? *(You can use a dictionary to help you.)*
d. Which is your favourite dance? Why? Can you do any of them?

UNIT 4 TRADITIONAL IRISH MUSIC

PART 1B WORLD INSTRUMENTS

1. What are the most famous musical instruments in the music of your country? *(Find a picture online to show your class.)*
2. Can you match each instrument below to the country they are from, to the pictures and to the audio?
   THE IRISH CULTURE BOOK - ONLINE SECTION: Book 3, Unit 4, Audio file 1. You'll hear the recording twice.

INSTRUMENT	COUNTRY	PICTURE	AUDIO
Guitar			
Bagpipes			
Sithar			
Vuvuzela			
Pandeiro			
Didgeridoo			
Lyre			
Ukulele			
Koto			

COUNTRY	Japan. South Africa. Scotland. Hawaii. Brazil. Australia. India. Spain. Greece.

3. Which instrument did you like the most?
4. Which instrument did you <u>not</u> like? Why?
5. Can you invent a new instrument? Work in pairs/small groups. Draw a picture of it.

PART 2A
TRADITIONAL IRISH MUSIC

Traditional Irish music is very popular both in Ireland and around the world.

In pairs/small groups, choose one of the types of Irish music below, answer the questions, and report back to the class.

a. People dance when they listen to Irish traditional music.
Listen to some traditional Irish music for dancing.
Which adjectives below describe this Irish music for dancing?
Slow. Fast. Sad. Energetic. Relaxing.
Do people dance to traditional music in your country?

b. Some traditional songs or 'balads' talk about Ireland's long history with England.
Listen to an Irish ballad online.
Do you think these songs are happy or sad songs?

c. 'Sean-nós' songs are old Irish songs. The singer sings the song with no musical instruments.
Listen to some 'Sean-nós' music. What do you think the singer is talking about in the song?

d. In the 19th and 20th centuries, millions of Irish people left Ireland and went to live in the USA, England, Australia etc. They brought Irish music with them. Are the sentences below True or False?
1. Irish traditional music sounds the same now as it did 200 years ago.
2. Irish traditional music has changed a lot. Irish music now uses modern instruments like, for example, the guitar.
Can you find any traditional Irish music online using a guitar?

e. A *seisiún* (ses-shoon) is a group of Irish people playing music together. Musicians often meet in a pub to play.
Look up a seisiún online and describe what you see.

UNIT 4 TRADITIONAL IRISH MUSIC

PART 2B IRISH INSTRUMENTS

1. Match the traditional Irish musical instruments below to the pictures and to the audio.
   THE IRISH CULTURE BOOK - ONLINE SECTION: Book 3, Unit 4, Audio file 2. You'll hear the recording twice.

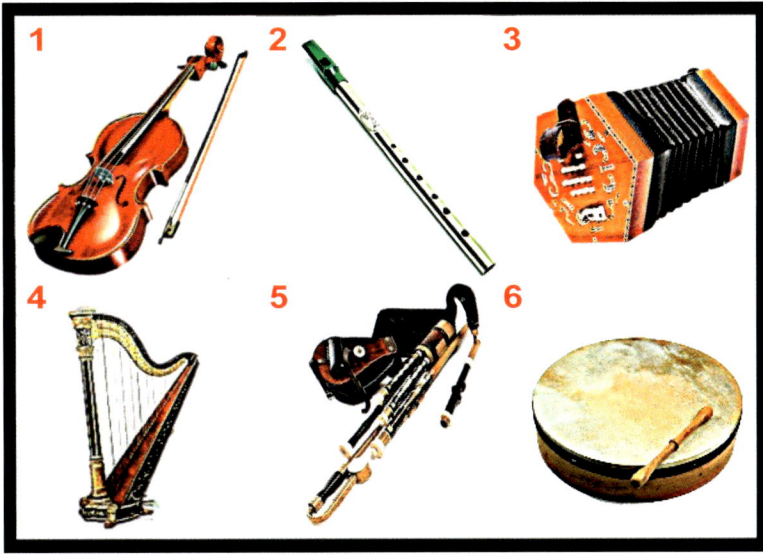

INSTRUMENT	PICTURE	AUDIO
Bodhrán (Bow-rawn)		
Fiddle/ Violin		
Tin Whistle		
Uilean Pipes (Ill-un)		
Concertina/ Accordion		
Harp		

2. Which instrument is your favourite?

PART 3 'WHISKEY IN THE JAR'

'Whiskey in the Jar' is one of the most popular Irish traditional songs.

1. The story of the song:

The song begins in the mountains in the south of Ireland. The singer steals money from an English soldier, Captain Farrell. The singer gives some of the money to his girlfriend Jenny but then Jenny helps the English soldiers. She puts water into the singer's gun. When the English soldiers arrive, the singer can't use his gun. He goes to prison. The singer is angry at Jenny. He hopes that his brother, who is also a soldier, will be able to help him.

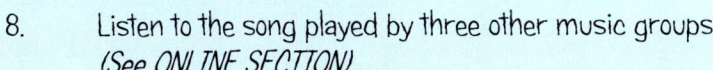

2. 'Whiskey in the Jar' is an old song and there are a lot of difficult words. Look in the ONLINE SECTION for the words of the song so you can read as you listen. There's also an explanation of some of the more difficult words.
   Remember – you don't need to understand all the words to enjoy the song.

3. Listen to the song by Irish group *The Dubliners.*

4. Do you like the song?

5. Is this a happy or sad song? Is it fast or slow? Is it energetic or relaxing?

6. Would you dance to this song or only listen to it?

7. Can you hear any of the instruments from PART 2B in the song? Look at the video online and check.

8. Listen to the song played by three other music groups.
   (See ONLINE SECTION).
   A. Irish rock group – *Thin Lizzy.*
   B. American heavy metal group – *Metallica.*
   C. Rock/folk group – *Grateful Dead.*
   Which do you like most?

9. Think of an old popular song from your country.
   Can play the song for your class? Can you explain the story of the song?

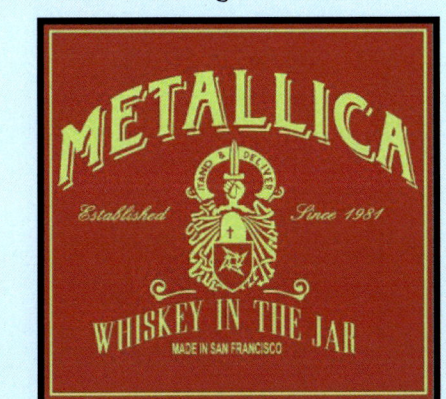

UNIT 4 TRADITIONAL IRISH MUSIC

PART 4 IRISH DANCING

1. What is the most famous traditional dance in your country? Can you do it?
2. Read the information below about traditional Irish dancing and answer the questions.
    A. Why did Irish people dance?
    B. Name two places where you can see Irish dancing today.
    C. What two types of shoes do you wear for Irish dancing?

HISTORY OF IRISH DANCING: In ancient Celtic times, Irish people danced together in circles. These dances were part of their religion, to celebrate and say thank you to their gods.
Ancient Irish people also danced to enjoy themselves and to have fun at social occasions.
Later, the dances became more complicated. Special dance teachers travelled around Ireland teaching people all the different moves.
In the 19th century, people danced together outside on the streets in the summer evenings. Today, Irish dancing is still popular at weddings and festivals.
There are also big competitions called 'feiseanna' where the best dancers in Ireland compete.

THE SHOES: There are two different types of shoes: hard and soft. Men only wear hard shoes. Women wear both.

THE DANCE: In Irish dancing you move your legs very quickly but you don't really move your arms. People usually dance in groups of four - two men and two women. The most simple step is '**one** two three, **one** two three…'

3. Watch some video of Irish dancing. *SEE ONLINE SECTION.* Can you see the dancer doing the 'one two three' step?
    NOW YOU - *Can you do the simple 'one two three' step? Try!*
4. One of the most popular group dances is 'The Walls of Limerick'. Watch it online and see if you can you do it as a class.
5. ***RIVERDANCE***

    Riverdance became famous in 1994 during the Eurovision Song Contest. The Riverdance show travelled all around the world, in Europe, Asia, America and Australia. It showed Irish dancing to more than 20 million people in more than 30 different countries. It was very popular.
    Watch 'Riverdance at the Eurovision' online.
    Do you like it? Why do you think it was so popular?

PART 5 AND FINALLY… MUSIC & LEARNING ENGLISH

Do you listen to music when you study? Does it help you to study?
Do you think it is good to use music in English class?

Music can…

- Help you remember English vocabulary
- Make learning English in class more fun
- Help you relax if you are stressed
- help you to understand difficult information

1. Do you agree with the sentences above?
2. Listen to some music. Close your eyes. Imagine that the music is from a new film that you are making. Imagine the situation in this new film. Who are the characters in the film? What are they doing? What are they talking about? Where are they? What is happening?
    Open your eyes. Write down everything you imagined. Now tell the other students about your film.
    Close your eyes again. listen to other types of music and imagine situations in different new films.

ON YOUR OWN

1. Go see a concert of traditional Irish music.
2. Learn how to sing an Irish song.
3. Learn how to play one song on an Irish musical instrument.

WARM UP

1. What types of music do you like most (rock/pop etc.)? Are there any types of music you <u>don't</u> like?
2. Who is your favourite music group or singer?
3. Do you listen to songs in English or only in your own language?
4. What is your favourite song at the moment?
5. Who are the most famous music groups/singers from your country?

PART 1 FIND SOMEONE WHO

Walk around your class. Talk to the other students. Find at least one student for each situation below.

FIND SOMEONE WHO…	STUDENT'S NAME	FURTHER INFORMATION
…<u>doesn't</u> listen to rock music.		*What music do they like?*
…knows two Irish singers or groups.		*Write the groups / singers here.*
…can sing.		*Write one song they can sing.*
…goes to music concerts.		*Which groups / singers?*
…knows two typical Irish musical Instruments.		*Write the instruments here.*
…has met a famous musician or singer.		*Who?*
…likes the same music group or singer as you.		*Which group / singer?*

QUOTES

Which is your favourite quote? Why?

"Music is very personal and spiritual. The music business is not spiritual. It is a business." – Van Morrison

"I feel hot, on fire, when I'm singing. I feel like a completely different person. It's very special." – Sinéad O'Connor

"For some people, listening to a song is better than going to a psychologist." – Dolores O'Riordan

"People write music because they are running to God or running away from God." – Bono, U2

"Music should be innocent and free." – Glen Hansard, The Frames

"I never wanted to be cool or famous. I just wanted to make great music." – Gavin Friday

"People sit and listen to music and they start to think about their life… Am I happy in my work? Am I happy in my relationships? What am I looking for?" – Enya

"You feel the love the audience has for you and you don't want it to end." – Phil Lynott

"The language of the planet is not English, it's music" – Bob Geldof

What do you think about the quotes? Can you think of any similar quotes from your culture?

PART 2A MUSIC GENRES

1. Can you match the styles of music on the left with the descriptions on the right?

A	REGGAE	Old-style music with lots of different instruments and a conductor.
B	ROCK	Loud, fast dance music.
C	HOUSE MUSIC	The singer speaks the words. Originally African-American music.
D	CLASSICAL	One of the most popular types of music. Lots of guitars and drums.
E	JAZZ	A music drama. The actors sing the words.
F	SINGER/SONGWRITER	The musicians can change the music each time they play.
G	RAP	Folk music from the south of the USA.
H	COUNTRY & WESTERN	Music written and sung by one musician often with guitar or piano.
I	OPERA	Music from Jamaica.

2. Now match each music style or genre above with the pictures below and the correct audio.
   THE IRISH CULTURE BOOK - ONLINE SECTION: Book 3, Unit 5, Audio file 1. You'll hear the recording twice.

PICTURE	MUSIC STYLE	AUDIO
1		
2		
3		
4		
5		
6		
7		
8		
9		

3. Which style of music do you like most? Which style of music do you <u>not</u> like?
4. Can you think of a famous singer/music group for each music style? *Look some up online if you don't know any.*
5. Can you sing in any of the music styles above? Do you want to sing now?!

PART 2B DESCRIBING MUSIC

Below are some expressions to talk about music.

In pairs or small groups, think of one example of a song for each expression.

– This song makes me happy if I'm sad.	– This is an old song but people still like it today.
– This is a very fast song. It gives me energy.	– I like this song but it is very sad.
– This song is very popular. Everybody knows it.	– When I listen to this song. I remember…

UNIT 5 MODERN IRISH MUSIC

PART 3A IRISH SINGERS

1. From the styles/image in each picture, can you match the Irish singers/music groups with the correct pictures?

SINGER/GROUP	PICTURE
Original Rudeboys *(Hip Hop)*	
Sinéad O'Connor *(Singer/Songwriter)*	
Enya *(Folk/New Age Melody)*	
The Cranberries *(Pop Rock)*	
The Pogues *(Celtic Punk)*	
The Irish Tenors *(Opera)*	
Westlife *(Boyband)*	
Van Morrison *(Soul/Blues/Jazz)*	
U2 *(Rock)*	

2. In pairs, choose one of the singers/groups. Look up three facts about them online and write them down. Find one of their most famous songs and listen to it. *(You can find some links in the ONLINE SECTION.) Do you like the song? Write down three adjectives to describe the song. (Use a dictionary to help you.) Report back to the class*
3. Find some music by a singer/group that you like from your country and play it for your class. Tell the other students why you like this music.

PART 3B IRISH MUSIC ALBUMS

Below is a list of ten famous Irish music albums.

A. **Read the description of each album. Choose one album that you would most like to listen to. Say why.**

1. **VAN MORRISON: ASTRAL WEEKS (1968)** This album was different from every other album at the time. It was a mix of jazz, soul and folk music.

2. **RORY GALLAGHER: LIVE IN EUROPE (1972)** Rory was a genius with the guitar. His music has a strong rock sound.

3. **THIN LIZZY: LIVE AND DANGEROUS (1978)** Great rock & roll. The singer Phil Lynnott has a deep, beautiful voice.

4. **THE POGUES: RUM, SODOMY & THE LASH (1986)** A mix of traditional Irish music and punk music. Lots of energy.

5. **ENYA: WATERMARK (1988)** A strange, magic album. Lots of old Celtic sounds and the lovely, soft voice of Enya.

Contd. on next page

PART 3B IRISH MUSIC ALBUMS *contd.*

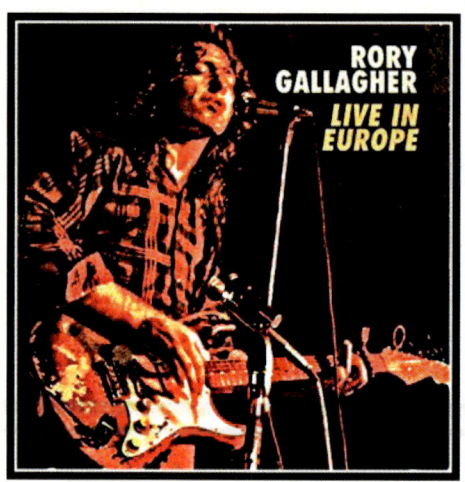

6. SINÉAD O'CONNOR: I DO NOT WANT WHAT I HAVEN'T GOT (1990) She has an ancient and beautiful voice. The words of the songs are really interesting.

7. U2: ACHTUNG BABY (1991) The biggest band in the world at the time. This album was something new for U2, an album that people could dance to.

8. THE CRANBERRIES: EVERYBODY ELSE IS DOING IT, SO WHY CAN'T WE (1993) A rock album about love and relationships and about feeling sad because of love.

9. THE FRAMES: FOR THE BIRDS (2001) Soft, slow songs. The instruments and the singing is beautiful. Lots of guitar and violin.

10. SNOW PATROL: EYES OPEN (2006) An album of perfect pop songs.

B.   Think of your own favourite album, a music album that you love.
      Can you write a short description (similar to above) of your album?
C.   Share your description with your class. Which of the other students' albums would you like to listen to?

PART 4 IRISH SONGS

Below are six of the singers/groups from the list of albums above. As a class, you must agree on one of these singers/groups you would like to listen to. Look up online to get more information on each one if you need.

> *U2. The Cranberries. Sinead O'Connor.*
>
> *The Frames. Snow Patrol. Van Morrison.*

In the *ONLINE SECTION,* you'll find a copy of the words of a song by the singer/group you've chosen. Some of the words of the song are missing.

a.   Listen to the song and fill in the gaps.
b.   Answer the questions about the song and read the quote by the artist about the song.

ON YOUR OWN

1.   Choose a singer/group that you like. Choose one of the options – a. b. or c – below.

a. Make a 'doodle' music video.

b. Make a 'literal' music video.

c. Make a 'Lip-synch' music video..

Show your videos to your class. Have a competition to choose which videos are the best.

2.   Imagine you are interviewing your favourite music star. Prepare the questions you would ask him/her. Role-play the interview with another student.

3.   Go to a music gig if you are in Ireland. There is a lot of good live music in Ireland. You might even see the next big Irish music star!

UNIT 6 A NICE CUPPA

WARM UP

1. What is your favourite drink?
2. Do you drink tea? How do you like it? (With lemon/milk/a biscuit?)
3. Look at the 'dingbat' below. A cup of tea **+** the famous American singer/actress Cher **=** ?

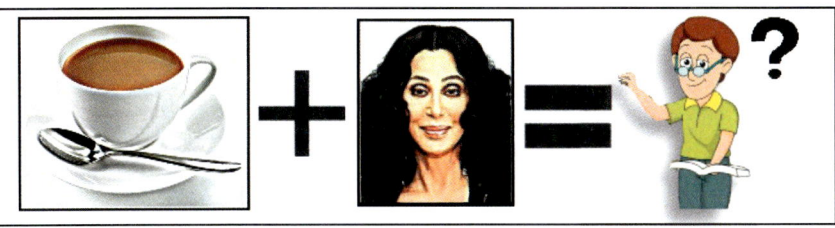

Hint: It's a person who could be important to you as a student.

PART 1A FAMOUS TEA DRINKERS
How many of the famous people drinking tea can you name?

PICTURE	TEA DRINKER'S NAME
1	
2	
3	
4	
5	
6	
7	
8	
9	

PART 1B THE A TO Z OF TEA

Useful 'tea' vocabulary:

Tea leaves	Loose tea	Tea bag	Kettle	Teapot

Read the A-Z of tea below.

1. *Most of the information below about tea is true. Four of the pieces of information are <u>not</u> true. Which four things do you think are false? Work in pairs or small groups.*

Astro-tea. Some people think you can use tea leaves to see the future.

Bags. Tea bags were invented in America by a team of scientists that included Albert Einstein.

Camellia sinensis is the scientific name for the tea plant.

Darjeeling. This is the 'champagne' of tea. It is very high quality.

Eat. Most people in Ireland like to drink tea with something to eat, usually a biscuit.

Feet. If your feet smell bad, put teabags on them. It will help.

Garden. Tea can help flowers grow faster in your garden.

Hot or cold. Iced tea is popular in the summer but most Irish people prefer hot tea.

India. Selling tea is the second biggest business in India.

Japan. The Japanese tea ceremony is very famous.

Kettle. You will see a kettle in almost every Irish kitchen.

Loose tea. Some people think loose tea tastes better than tea in a tea bag.

Mosquitoes. Tea leaves can protect you from mosquitoes.

Not just for drinking. Tea can be used as a medicine.

Overweight. Drinking tea can help make you thinner.

Party. The *Boston Tea Party* was not a party. It happened in the 1700s when Americans were fighting against the British.

Quotes. *"Women are like tea bags,"* said Eleanor Roosevelt. *"They don't know how strong they are until they are in hot water."*

Ritz Carlton, Hong Kong. This is the world's most expensive tea.

Speed. You get tea from a new tea plant after only two months.

Theanine. This ingredient in tea helps to make you calm.

Upper Class. In the past, only rich people drank tea in Ireland.

Versus Coffee. Tea has more caffeine than coffee.

Water. Tea is the second most popular drink in the world after water... People drink 3,000,000,000 cups of tea every year!

X-rated. Drinking tea can help improve your sex life.

Yu Lu The Chinese poet wrote the first tea book in the 8th century.

Zillah. The world's oldest petrol station is the *Teapot Dome Service Station* in Zillah, Washington, USA. It looks like a teapot.

2. *In your small groups, choose the three facts that you think are the most interesting. Share back with the class and say why.*
3. *Can you write some TRUE/FALSE facts about coffee or another drink that you like?*

PART 2A IRELAND AND TEA

1. *Which country do you think drinks the most coffee in the world?*
    A. Finland B. Italy C. USA
2. *Which country drinks the most tea?*
    A. England B. Ireland C. China

Read and discuss the questions below:

In Ireland, we drink much more tea than coffee.

– *Do people drink more tea or coffee in your country? What other drinks are popular?*

In the Irish language, the expression for 'a cup of tea' is *cupán tae*.

– *How do you say cup of tea in your language? Can you teach the other students to say it?*

Most people in Ireland put milk in their tea. 30% of people put sugar in their tea.

– *Have you tried tea with milk? How do people usually drink tea in your country?*

Tea in Ireland is very important. When you visit an Irish person in their home, they will offer you a cup of tea to welcome you.

– *If you visit a friend in their home in your country, will they offer you something to eat or drink when you arrive?*

In Ireland, people love to have time with friends for a chat and a good cup of tea.

– *What do you do when you want to have a long chat with a friend in your country?*

A young Bono enjoys a cup of tea

UNIT 6 A NICE CUPPA

PART 2B HOW TO MAKE A POT OF TEA

1. Learn how to make a perfect pot of tea in Ireland.
   Can you put the words in the sentences below in the correct order? Look at the pictures to help you.

1	kettle / with / Fill / water. / the
2	the kettle. / Heat / the water / in
3	hot water / a little / into the teapot. / Pour
4	two / tea bags / into the teapot. / Put / or three
5	for about two minutes. / the rest of the water / into the teapot / and wait / Pour
6	into your cup / Pour the tea / and add / if you want. / milk and sugar
7	Irish tea! / cup of / Enjoy / your perfect

2. In pairs, can you write the instructions for how to make the 'perfect cup of coffee' or another drink you like?

PART 3A TIME FOR TEA
FIVE SITUATIONS FOR TEA IN IRELAND

1. If you have broken up with your boyfriend/girlfriend. Talk to your mother about it with a cup of tea.

2. When your friend or your neighbour visits your house.

3. Having a chat or gossip with your friend.

4. If you went out to a pub last night and you feel very tired today.

5. After a hard day working or studying. relax with tea and a biscuit.

– *Make a list of 3 situations when you would drink a coffee or another drink that you like.*

PART 3B SAYING NO TO TEA IN IRELAND (NO?)

When you visit an Irish person's home. they almost always offer you a cup of tea. Have you ever experienced how difficult it is to say no to a tea in Ireland? What should you do if you really don't want a cup of tea? *See below.*

One of the most famous Irish TV comedy characters was the housekeeper Mrs Doyle from the series *Father Ted.*. She was always offering people tea even when they didn't want it. *(If possilbe. watch Mrs. Doyle's character online.)*

Can you tell the class about a famous TV comedy character in your country?
(If possible. show the class some video of this character online.)

Mrs. Doyle's 'catchphrase' (the thing she always said) was *'Ah. go on. go on.'* What do you think it means? Does the famous TV comedy character in your country have a catchphrase?

In pairs, can you invent your own TV character and give them a catchphrase?

* *Sometimes it's better to take a tea even if you don't really want it and just drink a little bit. People like to give you something to make you feel welcome.*

'Ah. go on…'

PART 4
HOW <u>NOT</u> TO MAKE A CUP OF TEA

You can make tea without a teapot, with a tea bag directly into your cup. It should be simple, but…

This is Michael. He loves tea but he gets a bit angry when people don't make his tea the way he likes it.

Why is Michael unhappy in each situation below?

In pairs/small groups, can you match each picture with the tea-making mistakes below?

PICTURE	TEA-MAKING MISTAKE
	Leaving the tea bag in the cup.
	Only putting the tea bag into the water for a moment. The tea is not strong enough.
	Using a tea bag more than once.
	Putting the milk in first.
	Not making a full cup of tea. Only using half of the cup.
	Leaving the spoon in the cup.

A FINAL FEW THOUGHTS

1. If you want to be 'posh' when you drink tea, put your little finger like in the picture below. Try it yourself!

2. MIFFY or TIFFY? This is a big debate!

   MIFFY means that you put the milk into the cup first and then you put the tea.

   TIFFY means you put the tea in the cup first and then put in the milk.

   Is Michael a MIFFY or TIFFY person? (What are you?)

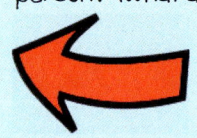

ON YOUR OWN

1. Watch an episode of *Father Ted*. Look for Mrs Doyle.
2. Share a cup of tea and have a chat with a friend.
3. Ask an Irish person how and when they like to drink tea.
4. Tea Culture in the World.

   Choose one culture: e.g. Indian / Chinese / Korean / English etc. Research how people drink tea in that country.
5. Advertising for tea –

   Find some Irish TV ads for tea online. In pairs/small groups, create your own ads for drinking coffee, hot chocolate or another drink. Show them to the class.

WARM UP

1. Why are you learning English - for your job/travel etc.?
2. Do you think English is a difficult language to learn? Is it more difficult or easier to learn than your language?
3. Do you think Irish people's accent is difficult to understand?

TEST YOUR KNOWLEDGE:
Four questions about the English language

a. *How many words are there in the English language?*
b. *What is the most commonly used letter in English?*
c. *What is the most commonly used word in English?*
d. *What is the most commonly sung song in English?*

PART 1A ENGLISH AND THE WORLD

1. English has imported many words from other languages. Match each word below with its original language.

Vodka		Jeans	
Skiing		Philosophy	
Taekwando		Guitar	
Umbrella		Paper	
Tsunami		Kiwi	
Kangaroo		Hamburger	

A. Italian B. Spanish C. Russian D. French E. Greek
F. Norwegian G. Maori (New Zealand) H. Japanese I. German
J. Korean K. Aborigine (Australia) L. Egyptian

2. Is your language included above? Can you find any words from your language that are used in English?
3. English also exports words to other languages. Are there any English words used in your language?

PART 1B IRISH AND THE WORLD

Two words that were imported into English from Ireland are *'whiskey'* and *'hooligan'*.

1. Find the meaning of the original Irish word for *whiskey*.
2. Look up the Irish family name which *hooligan* comes from.

Whiskey	Hooligan

3. Do you know any words in the Irish language? *Look some up.*

QUOTES

Which is your favourite quote? Why?

"If you could teach the English how to talk and the Irish how to listen, there would be no problems between the two countries."
– Oscar Wilde

"For an Irishman, talking is like a dance."
– Deborah Love

"When the eyes of people speak to you, you don't need a dictionary to understand. The language is the same in all the world."
– Ralph Waldo Emmerson

"Britain and America are two countries who have the same language but who don't understand each other."
– G.B. Shaw

"Irish is the perfect language to talk to someone who is sad and make them happy." – J.M. Synge

"The limits of my language are the limits of my world." – Wittgenstein

"Your facial expression is the most important thing you wear."
– Janet Lane

"The language of friendship is not words but kind actions." – Henry Thoreau

"The body says what words cannot."
– Claire Kelly

What do you think about the quotes? Can you think of any similar quotes from your culture?

'That film was deadly!'

'Deadly? What do you mean? Was it violent?'

UNIT 7 HOW IRISH PEOPLE COMMUNICATE

PART 2A 'AS GAEILGE' - THE IRISH LANGUAGE

1. There are differences in how people speak English in Ireland compared to, for example, Britain or America. Can you correct the 'mistakes' in the colloquial Irish sentences below?
   The sentences below are all influenced by the Irish language, *Gaeilge*.

A. I'm doing it wrong, ***amn't I***?	
B. Where's ***me*** mobile phone?	
C. What ***does he be doing*** up in his room?	
D. What are ***ye*** doing for the weekend?	
E. ***Youse*** don't understand anything.	

2. Have you noticed anything else different about how Irish people speak English?
3. Can you translate one colloquial expression you really like from your language into English?

PART 2B UNDERSTANDING MEANING FROM CONTEXT

1. People in Ireland often use some of the expressions below. What do you think the words in ***bold/italics*** mean? Choose option **A** or **B** for each one. *Use the context of the sentences to help you.*

1. 'He's a ***gas*** man! I love talking to him.'	**A.** Funny **B.** Stupid
2. 'How was your weekend?' '***Deadly!*** We visited the Cliffs of Moher.'	**A.** Very good **B.** Very bad
3. 'How is your new job?' 'Ah, it's ***grand***. It's a job.'	**A.** Big **B.** OK
4. 'Was there any ***craic*** at the party?' 'Yeah, I had a nice time.'	**A.** Fun **B.** Drugs
5. 'Who is ***yer man***?'	**A.** That guy **B.** Your father
6. '***C'mere,*** how was your holiday?''	**A.** Listen **B.** Go away
7. 'How was the weather?' '***Brutal.*** It rained all day.'	**A.** Very good **B.** Very bad

'Any craic at the party?'

'What type of parties do you think I go to?'

2. Can you make your own sentences using some of the expressions?

PART 3 HOW IRISH SOUND - INTERJECTIONS

1. ONLINE SECTION: Book 3 Audio file 1.
   Can you listen and match the 'interjection sounds' in the box with their meanings below?

Yay! -- Sshh -- Huh? -- Argh -- Yuck -- Aha, aha   Ouch -- Oh? -- Brrr -- Oops -- Mwah -- Aah, OK   Uh oh -- HaHa -- Em/eh/um -- Mmmm

Yuk!

Ooops!

Surprise		I understand		Be quiet		Tastes bad	
Pain		We're in trouble		I'm happy		My mistake	
A kiss		I'm thinking		I don't understand		I'm cold	
I'm angry		That's funny		Tastes good		I'm listening	

2. Practise using some of the interjection sounds above. (Your teacher can give you some example situations.)
3. Can you think of any interjection sounds in your language? Are they different or similar to English?

UNIT 7 HOW IRISH PEOPLE COMMUNICATE

PART 4A GESTURES QUIZ

Body language and gestures are an important part of how we speak and communicate.
TEST WHAT YOU KNOW ABOUT GESTURES FROM AROUND THE WORLD.

1. In what country is it rude to sit so that people can see the bottom of your feet?
    A. Ireland
    B. Canada
    C. Vietnam

2. If you you make the 'rabbit ears' sign (as in the picture) to a Brazilian or Italian man, what are you saying to him?
    A. That he is going bald
    B. That his wife is having a relationship with another man
    C. That he is ugly

3. In Greece a downward movement or nod of your head means 'yes'. An upward nod means 'no'. What other gesture is used in Greece to say 'yes'?
    A. Thumb up finger point
    B. Moving your head from side to side
    C. Touching your nose

4. Irish people use the 'OK' sign (as in the picture) to say everything is good. What would a person from Saudi Arabia understand by this gesture?
    A. You're saying they are stupid
    B. You're saying you have no money
    C. You're giving them the 'evil eye' (Saying something bad will happen to them)

5. How do you gesture for someone to come to you in Japan?
    A. Palm down hand movement
    B. Palm up hand movement
    C. Touching your eye

6. Can you match the meaning of sticking out your tongue with the correct 'culture' below?

    A. Ireland   *1. Aggression*
    B. Tibet   *2. An insult (for children)*
    C. New Zealand   *3. Joking/Flirting*
    D. Sending a text *4. Welcome/Respect*

7. The 'V' sign usually means 'peace' or 'victory' (Picture A). In Ireland, with the back of the hand to the other person (Picture B), what does it mean?
    A. To say you love someone
    B. To ask someone for help
    C. To insult someone

a. **Do you know any other gestures from around the world?**
b. **Can you demonstrate a typical gesture from your country?**

PART 4B BODY LANGUAGE

SAYING HELLO: Which way in the box below do you use to say hello to someone in your country?

> *A. Kisses on the cheeks B. Shaking hands C. Embracing D. Bowing E. Something else*

1. Do you say hello in a different way to a boy or to a girl? Is it different to somebody older vs somebody younger than you?
2. Do Irish people say hello in the same way as in your country?

PHYSICAL CONTACT: Can you write down one situation in which you would use the types of physical contact in the box below?

> *A. Holding hands B. Linking arms C. A high five*
> *D. An arm around the shoulder E. A pat on the head*

1. Do you think Irish people use more or less physical contact than in your culture?

37

PART 4B BODY LANGUAGE *contd.*

INTERPERSONAL DISTANCE:

1. How would you describe the relationship between the two people in the pictures **A B** & **C** below? (Is it a work relationship? Are they friends or family? Are they boyfriend/girlfriend?)

A  **B**  **C**

2. Do Irish people stand closer or further away when they're talking to you than people in your culture?
3. If there are other nationalities in your class, stand up and have conversation together. How close do you stand to each other? Is your 'interpersonal distance' the same or different?

EXTROVERT OR INTROVERT:

1. Look at the pictures below. Do you think you are more similar to the extrovert or the introvert person? Compare your answer with a partner. Which one of you is more extrovert or introvert?

EXTROVERT

She is social

She likes being in groups

She has a big group of friends

She likes doing new activities

INTROVERT

He is private emotionally

He likes to observe and think about life

He likes being alone

He is shy

2. In which countries are people generally more 'social' and where are people generally more 'reserved and shy'? Compare your ideas with a partner.
3. Do you think people from your culture are generally more social or reserved compared to Irish people?

AND FINALLY… Can you write down two ways in which people move differently in general in your country compared to Ireland? E.g. Do they walk more quickly or more slowly?

ON YOUR OWN

1. In the book *The Meaning of Liff*, the writer Douglas Adams invents names for 'common experiences and situations for which no words exist.'

   Some of the words he invented include:

ABINGER (n.) Someone who washes up everything except the frying pan.
BANFF (adj.) The facial expression you make in your passport photograph.
FIUNARY (n.) The safe place you put something and then forget where it was.

   Can *you* invent some words for these situations?
   - The feeling after months of studying that your English is getting worse.
   - The expression Irish people make when they look up at the sky on a rainy day.
   - The look a teacher gives to a student who has arrived late for class (again!)
   - The smile a teacher gives a student who makes a grammatically correct sentence.

2. What other things do you think we need new words for? In pairs/small groups, invent some new words.

UNIT 8 IRISH WEATHER

WARM UP

1. What is your favourite type of weather?
2. What weather do you <u>not</u> like?
3. How is Irish weather different from your country?
4. If you are in Ireland now, look out the window. How would you describe the weather?

PART 1 WEATHER VOCABULARY

Is the vocabulary vocabulary below used more for winter or summer or used for both? Can you put each word in the correct column?

WEATHER VOCABULARY
Cold – Hot – Rainy – Sunny – Wet – Cool – Windy – Dry
Snowy – Storm – Rainbow – Thunder & Lightning
Showers – Hailstones – Ice – Freezing – Warm – Breeze
Fog – Frost – Humid – Boiling – Clear – Cloudy

WINTER	SUMMER	BOTH

1. Which of the words in the box are nouns and which are adjectives? Mark the words 'N' for noun or 'A' for adjective.
2. Which words would you associate with Irish weather?
3. Match the symbols with the types of weather below.

Cloudy		Thunderstorm	
Heavy Rain		Heavy Snow	
Sunshine		Rain Showers	
Light Rain		Sleet	

4. Can you draw symbols for any other types of weather? Get the other students to say what type of weather each one is.

39

PART 2A DESCRIBE IRISH WEATHER

"If you don't like the weather in Ireland, don't worry, wait a few minutes and it will change."

1. The Irish climate is often described as *'changeable'*. What do you think *'changeable'* means?
2. In Ireland, we sometimes have *'four seasons in one day'*. What do you think this means?
3. How would you describe the climate in your country?
4. Irish people talk a lot about the weather so they need a lot of different weather vocabulary and expressions.

    Can you match the Irish weather descriptions on the left to the type of weather on the right?

A	*"It's perfect weather for ducks."*	1	It has stopped raining
B	*"It's Arctic out there."*	2	Warm weather with a breeze
C	*"God is moving his furniture upstairs."*	3	Stay inside, the weather is horrible
D	*"It's a good day to sit beside the fire or go to the pub."*	4	It's a very hot sunny day
E	*"You could fry an egg on the stones."*	5	It's freezing cold
F	*"It's a good day for drying your washed clothes."*	6	There is a thunderstorm
G	*"There's a break in the weather."*	7	It's raining a lot

A	B	C	D	E	F	G

5. Which expression is your favourite?
6. Can you think of any similar expressions for weather in your language?

PART 2B THE IRISH INVENTED WIND

1. *'How strong is the wind?'* An Irishman Francis Beaufort invented the scientific way to describe wind.
    Can you match the wind descriptions in the box with the Beaufort scale categories on the right below?

WIND DESCRIPTIONS	A. Everything is destroyed – houses, trees etc. B. You can feel a soft breeze on your face. C. Large tree branches move D. Small tree branches begin to move E. Big trees fall onto the ground F. It is difficult to walk against the wind

BEAUFORT CATEGORIES	DESCRIPTIONS
2 Light Breeze *(6–11 kmph)*	
4 Moderate Breeze *(21–30 kmph)*	
6 Strong Breeze *(41–50 kmph)*	
8 Gale *(61–74 kmph)*	
10 Storm *(85–100 kmph)*	
12 Hurricane *(115 kmph +)*	

2. Can you invent a scale like this for other weather types – for rain or sun?

UNIT 8 IRISH WEATHER

PART 3A WHAT DO YOU KNOW ABOUT THE WEATHER?
WEATHER QUIZ
In pairs/small groups, how many questions can you answer?

1. Which do we see/hear first – thunder or lightning? _____

2. How many colours are there in the rainbow? (How many can you name?)
   _____

3. Dublin is the place in Ireland that has the most rain. **True/False**

4. The sunniest area of Ireland is Wexford in the south-east. **True/False**

5. Ireland is one of the safest places in the world from earthquakes. **True/False**

6. North winds normally bring warm weather to Ireland. **True/False**

7. Most of Ireland's rain comes from the Atlantic Ocean. **True/False**

8. In the winter, most of the rivers in Ireland freeze with ice. **True/False**

9. What are the three months of summer in Ireland? (And winter?) _____

10. On what date is the longest day of the year in Ireland? (And the shortest day?) _____

11. Irish scientist, John Tyndall, discovered the 'greenhouse effect'. What is the 'greenhouse effect'?
    _____

12. What weather does 'Low Pressure' usually mean for Ireland? (And 'High'?) _____

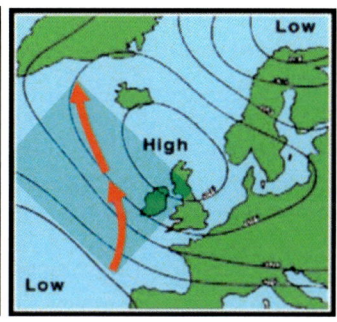

In pairs/small groups, can you make any more questions about the weather in general or the weather in your country? Ask the other students.

PART 3B DISCUSS IRISH WEATHER

1. In pairs or small groups discuss the weather questions in the box. Can you write an answer for each one?

A. Why do you think the Equator is hotter than the North and South Poles?

B. Why is Dublin usually much warmer in winter than Moscow? The two cities are on almost the same latitude but the average January temperatures are Dublin: 3°C. Moscow: −16°C.

C. Why does it rain so much in Ireland?

D. What clothes should you bring if you're visiting Ireland?

E. Why do Irish people talk a lot about the weather?

2. Weather affects the type of houses we live in. Are houses in Ireland different in from your country?

3. Weather affects the clothes we wear. Do Irish people dress differently from in your country?

PART 4 NOW YOU - BECOME A WEATHER FORECASTER

METHOD 1: LOOK AT THE SKY

Is good or bad weather coming? Match each weather sign in the sentences with the symbol of the weather that is coming on the right.

A. Look at the clouds.
1. The clouds are low and dark.
2. The clouds are high and white.

B. Look for a red sky.
3. There is a red sky in the evening (sunset).
4. There is a red sky in the morning (sunrise).

C. Look for a rainbow.
5. The rainbow is in the west in the morning.
6. The rainbow is in the east in the evening.

* Can you think of the explanations behind the weather signs?

METHOD 2: FEEL THE WIND AND AIR

A. Throw a piece of grass in the air to check wind direction.
1. The wind is from the west (the Atlantic).
2. The wind is from the east.
3. The wind is strong.

B. Check if the grass is dry or wet early in the morning.
4. The grass is dry in the morning.
5. The grass is wet (with dew) in the morning.

C. Close your eyes, take a deep breath and smell the air.
6. There is a strong smell of plants and nature.

* Can you think of the explanations behind the weather signs?

METHOD 3: WATCHING ANIMAL BEHAVIOUR

A. Look at cows in a field.
1. Cows are lying down or are close together.

B. Take note of the birds.
2. The birds are flying high in the sky.
3. The birds are flying low in the sky.

ON YOUR OWN

1. Watch a weather forecast on TV. What can you understand?
2. Make videos of your own weather forecasts and show them to your class. Vote for the best one.

'The weather is very bad at the moment...' - Boy

'Are you really talking about the weather on a first date?' - Girl

'I'm sorry, I don't think this is going to work.' - Girl

UNIT 9 IRISH LEGENDS & LITERATURE

WARM UP

1. Do you read? Are you reading a book now?
2. What kinds of books do you usually like/dislike?
3. What was your favourite fairy story as a child?
4. Who is your favourite modern superhero?
5. Do you know any famous legends from your culture?

PART 1 LEGEND CHARACTERS

1. Can you match the typical characters from legend stories in the box to the pictures and the descriptions?

CHARACTER TYPE	1	2	3	4	5	6
PICTURE						
DESCRIPTION						

> **1.** The action girl **2.** The old teacher **3.** The bad queen
> **4.** The hero **5.** The friendly monster **6.** The enemy

A. He is strong and good and he fights to protect people
B. She is independent and full of energy. She fights for freedom
C. He is intelligent and wise. He gives advice to the hero
D. She is beautiful but also dangerous with magic power
E. The bad character trying to kill the hero
F. He looks scary but he helps the hero against the enemy

2. Can you think of any examples of the characters above in legends or in modern stories?
3. Look at the descriptions below. Can you think of examples of each character in modern fantasy or superhero films? Look them up online.

Antihero	A hero who also has lots of bad characteristics
Wizard	A man (usually old) who has magical powers
Shape-shifter	Someone who can completely change how they look

4. Working in pairs/small groups, can you write a short description for each of the characters in the box below?

> A bad king -- Witches -- A dangerous rival to the hero

I am a legend. If you don't believe me, just ask me.

IRISH LAKE GIANT

43

UNIT 9 IRISH LEGENDS & LITERATURE

PART 2 IRISH HEROES: CÚ CHULAINN & FIONN MACCUMHAILL

1. Work in pairs. Each student should read one of the stories about the two most famous heroes of Irish legend, *Cú Chulainn* and *Fionn MacCumhaill*. Tell your partner the two most interesting things that you learn.

CÚ CHULAINN was the son of a god and a normal woman. His uncle Conchobar was the King of **Ulster**. When Cú Chulainn was sixteen, Queen Medb of **Connacht** attacked Ulster and tried to steal their best bull. Cú Chulainn fought alone against all the Connacht army at **Cooley** and won. When Cú Chulainn was fighting, he became crazy and changed into a scary monster. His legs turned backwards, his eyes came out of his head and his mouth grew big teeth. After one fight, his friends threw him into a bath of ice water to calm him down but the bath exploded!

Cú Chulainn wanted to marry **Emer**. Emer's father **Forgall** told Cú Chulainn he must first go to Scotland and fight the famous warrior-woman, **Scáthach**. Forgall hoped that Scáthach would kill Cú Chulainn. When Cú Chulainn fought Scáthach, they were equally strong. Later Scáthach became pregnant with Cú Chulainn's son. While she was pregnant, Cú Chulainn returned to Ireland, killed Forgall and married Emer. Eight years later, Scáthach sent the young Connla to Ireland in secret. Cú Chulainn killed him. He only understood at the last moment that Connla was his son.

On his way to fight a group of men, Cú Chulainn met **The Morrigan**, three horrible old women with one eye each. They invited him to eat with them. They put special magic in his food to make him weak during the fight. Cú Chulainn was killed at **Knockbridge, County Louth**. As he was dying, he tied himself to a rock so he died standing up, looking at his enemies.

FIONN MACCUMHAILL lived as a young boy in secret in the **Slieve Bloom mountains**. His father was killed by **Goll**, an important king in Ireland. Goll was looking for Fionn to kill him too. Fionn studied with an old magician **Finnegas** who taught him many secrets and also how to fight.

Finnegas was looking for the famous 'salmon of knowledge' in the **River Boyne**. When Finnegas finally caught the fish, he told Fionn to cook it for him. While cooking, Fionn burned his finger on the fish and put his finger in his mouth. Fionn then got all the salmon's knowledge and intelligence. Fionn was now strong enough to fight against Goll. Fionn became the new, good king in Ireland.

Fionn's first wife was **Sadbh**. When he first saw her, she was a deer running in the forest. When Fionn touched her, she changed into a beautiful woman. They had one son, Oisín. Later, Sadbh changed back into a deer and disappeared into the forest.

Fionn once threw a piece of land into the sea at an enemy. The big hole became the lake, **Lough Neagh**. Fionn also created the **Giant's Causeway** as a bridge from Ireland to Scotland.

When Fionn learned that the Scottish giant **Benandonner** wanted to fight him, Fionn was afraid. He knew he couldn't win so he asked his second wife Oona to dress him as a baby. When Benandonner arrived and saw how big and strong the 'baby' was, he ran back to Scotland.

1. Which legend/hero is your favourite? Why?
2. Can you find the places from the two legend stories in the box below on a modern map of Ireland? *(You can look up the places online.)*

> *Ulster & Connacht – Cooley – Knockbridge – Slieve Bloom Mountains*
> *River Boyne – Lough Neagh – Giant's Causeway*

3. In the grid below, can you match the typical character types (from the page before) with the specific characters from the two Irish legends?

ANTI-HERO	A. Cú Chulainn or B. Fionn
ACTION GIRL	A. Sadbh or B. Scáthach
SHAPE-SHIFTER	A. Sadbh or B. Scáthach
MAGIC WIZARD	A. Finnegas or B. Benandonner
THE OLD TEACHER	A. Goll or B. Finnegas
DANGEROUS RIVAL	A. Emer or B. Benandonner
THE BAD KING	A. The Morrigan or B. Goll
WITCHES	A. The Morrigan or B. Forgall

4. In pairs/small groups, can you invent your own legend hero? Compare with other groups and vote on the best one.
5. If you were a modern superhero, what powers would you have? Ask the other students also.

UNIT 9 IRISH LEGENDS & LITERATURE

PART 3 'LABHRAIDH LOINGSEACH'

1. Look at the picture of Labhraidh Loinseach, an ancient, legendary High King of Ireland. You might notice that he has horse's ears. In pairs/small groups, invent your own answers to the questions below to create your own story.

1. *How did Labhraidh get his horse's ears?*
2. *How did he keep his ears secret?*
3. *What was the problem with getting his hair cut?*
4. *What do you think happened to all his hairdressers?*
5. *What did one hairdresser offer Labhraidh that Labhraidh accepted?*
6. *Where did this hairdresser go to whisper the secret of the horses ears?*
7. *Why did the king want to have a big celebration after ten years?*
8. *Where did the musician go to find wood to make a new harp?*
9. *What happened when the musician played the harp at the celebration?*
10. *What did the king do?*

2. Compare your stories with other groups. Ask your teacher or check the ONLINE SECTION for the full story.

PART 4 IRISH WRITERS

1. Four Irish writers have won the Nobel Prize for Literature - **WB Yeats, George Bernard Shaw, Samuel Beckett** and **Seamus Heaney**. Do you know any other famous Irish writers? *Look them up online.*
2. Who are the most famous writers from your country?
3. Answer the questions about four other famous Irish writers using the information in the boxes below.

A. Which two writers didn't live in Ireland?

B. Which writers wrote plays, poems, novels and stories for children?

Plays	Poems	Novels	Stories for Children

C. Which writer(s) created a very famous character?

Jonathan Swift (1667-1745) was religious dean in St. Patrick's Cathedral, Dublin. He was a poet and novelist. He had a famous secret relationship with a woman named 'Stella'. His most famous work is *Gulliver's Travels.* Before he died, he gave his all money to open a mental hospital in Dublin.
Oscar Wilde (1854-1900) lived in London and wrote popular plays which were full of upper-class English people in ridiculous situations. His plays were very funny and clever. He also wrote children's stories. When he was very famous, he went to prison for a sexual scandal.
Bram Stoker (1847-1912) studied maths in Trinity College, Dublin. He married Oscar Wilde's ex-girlfriend. He spent eight years studying European legends, especially vampires. His most famous novel was *Dracula.*
James Joyce (1882-1941) lived most of his adult life in Treviso, Italy and Paris, France. Joyce thought Ireland was too small and narrow-minded for him to live in but he returned to Dublin in his imagination. His most famous novels, including *Dubliners* and *Ulysses,* took place in Dublin.

1. *Who is who? Can you match the writers above to their pictures?*

UNIT 9 IRISH LEGENDS & LITERATURE

PART 5 FIRST LINES

1. Can you match the first line of each book with the book covers below?

A.	'Secret agent Jane Green knew she had to stop General Kurt and his team of criminals from taking control of the world's water. She also knew she was in a race against time to save the world…'
B.	'The first thing you need to know about me is that I'm not a leprechaun. Ok?! I'm a faery king. And, you also need to know that it's not easy being a secret faery king in this modern world of social media…'
C.	'The police didn't believe Julia when she said her neighbour was murdered. She left the police station. She was beginning to understand that she couldn't trust anyone, especially the police…'
D.	'Denise O'Gara was a young, pretty nurse. She lived in Dublin in a flat with two friends from school. She was looking for love but it was difficult to find in 21st century Ireland…'
E.	'Jimbo was different. He didn't have any friends among the other elephants. His best friends were a young girl called Sally and her brother Brendan. It was them who gave him his first hat…'

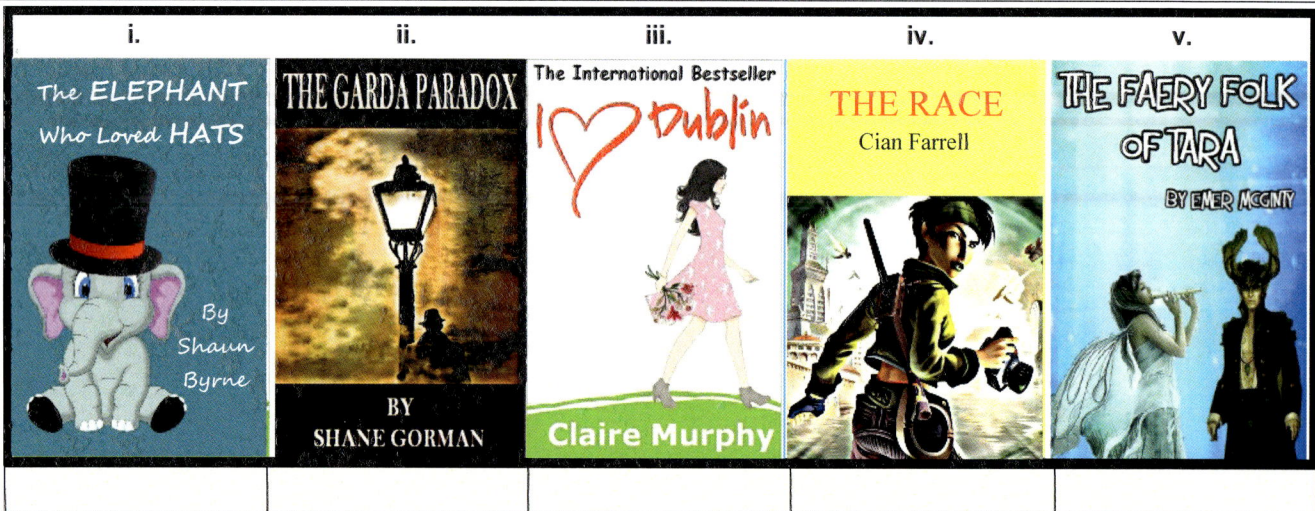

i.	ii.	iii.	iv.	v.

2. Can you match each book to a genre in the boxes?

1. Crime Thriller		**2.** Romantic Drama		**3.** Children's Book		**4.** Fantasy		**5.** Action Adventure	

3. Which book above would you most like to read?

4. Can you write what you think the story of the book will be? *Where does it take place? What happens? Who are the main characters? etc.* Present your story to the class. (Ask your teacher for the real story.)

5. Can you think of other examples of books for each genre? Do you know any other genres of books?

6. Think of a book you love. Show the first line to your class. If possible, also show the book cover. If the other students don't know the book, can they say what it will be about? Say why you love this book.

ON YOUR OWN

1. Write a short story, starting with one of these lines:

It was midnight…
He walked slowly home from the party…
She was afraid…

2. If you're in Dublin – visit the Dublin Writers Museum, the Joyce Tower, Oscar Wilde Statue or St. Patrick's Cathedral where Swift is buried.

3. If you're in Sligo, visit Yeats' tomb.

4. Write a review of a book you love and present it to your class.

5. Read a book in English.

6. Watch a film about Irish legends like *The Song of the Sea.*

7. Invent a legend to explain: Why it rains in Ireland? Why Irish have red hair? How the Irish invented whiskey? etc.

8. Visit Tara.. or Newgrange. or other ancient places associated with legends in Ireland.

WARM UP

1.   Do you like sport? Which sport is your favourite?
2.   What is the most popular sport in your country?
3.   Who is your favourite sportsperson?
4.   Do you know any Irish sports?

PART 1 'FASTER, HIGHER, STRONGER'

1.   TRIVIA QUESTION: What colour are the five Olympic rings?
2.   Which Olympic sports is your country best at?
3.   Which Olympic sports do you think Ireland is best at?
4.   Can you match the Olympic sports with the symbols below?

OLYMPIC SPORT	SYMBOL	OLYMPIC SPORT	SYMBOL
Badminton		Ice Hockey	
Kayaking		Swimming	
Judo		Diving	
Volleyball		Athletics	
Weightlifting		Archery	
Handball		Table Tennis	
Boxing		Cycling	
Gymnastics		Skiing	

5.   Have you played any of the sports above?
6.   Which of the sports above would you most like to try?
7.   Can you design symbols for some of the sports in the box below (or other sports)? Get other students to guess the sport.

> Football – Basketball – Baseball – Tennis – Long Jump
> Hockey – Rugby – High Jump – Snowboarding – Golf

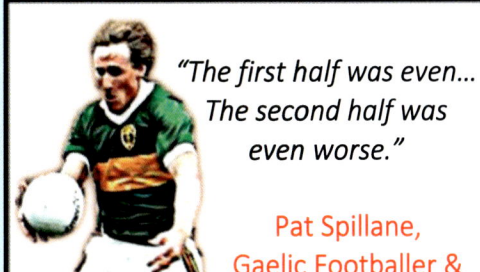

"The first half was even... The second half was even worse."

Pat Spillane, Gaelic Footballer & TV Commentator

PART 2A GAELIC GAMES

1. Ireland's national sports (Gaelic games) are Gaelic football, hurling, camogie and handball.
   In pairs, decide if you think the facts below are TRUE or FALSE.

GAA FACTS	T/F
Gaelic footballers earn a lot of money for playing football	
Hurling has been played in Ireland for about one hundred years	
Ireland play Gaelic football internationals against Australia	
The Gaelic Games stadium Croke Park is the third biggest in Europe	
The rules of hurling were originally copied from ice hockey	
The USA sports channel ESPN voted 'The Top Ten Best Sport Events To Watch Live': 1. The Olympic 100 metres final. 2. The football World Cup final **3. The All-Ireland hurling final**	

2. What is the national sport in your country? Can you make some TRUE or FALSE facts about it and ask your class?
3. **HOW TO PLAY:** Watch some video of Gaelic football and hurling. *(See ONLINE SECTION.)*
   Can you match the Rules below to the correct sport? *Look up any difficult words in a dictionary.*

A. Games are seventy minutes long **B.** It's like a mix of rugby and soccer **C.** Teams of fifteen players **D.** You hit the ball with a stick **E.** Ball over the bar = one point / Ball into the goal = three points **F.** It's like hockey but you can touch the ball with your hands **G.** As you run, bounce the ball or drop it onto your foot **H.** Kick the ball to pass and to score **I.** As you run, balance the ball on the stick

Point

Goal

GAELIC FOOTBALL		HURLING		BOTH	

4. Write out the rules for another sport - the other students must guess which sport it is.
5. If you have a ball for Gaelic football or a hurl and sliothar, practice some Gaelic games skills for yourself!

PART 2B IRISH SPORTING GREATS

1. Can you match the pictures with the famous Irish sportspeople and with their achievements?

SPORTSPERSON
1. Sean Kelly – *Cycling*
2. Henry Shefflin – *Hurling*
3. Brian O'Driscoll – *Rugby*
4. Robbie Keane – *Football*
5. Sonia O'Sullivan – *Athletics*
6. Katie Taylor – *Boxing*

ACHIEVEMENT
A. Scored forty-six tries for Ireland
B. All-Ireland champion ten times
C. 5000 metres Olympic silver medal
D. Won Tour of Spain
E. Scored sixty-eight goals for Ireland
F. Olympic lightweight champion

PICTURE	i	ii	iii	iv	v	vi
SPORTSPERSON						
ACHIEVEMENT						

2. Which achievement do you think is the best? Find out more about the sportsperson you like most.
3. Who is the best or most famous sportsperson in your country?
4. In small groups, share your own personal 'best' sporting achievement? (It can be big or small!)

UNIT 10 IRISH SPORT & LEISURE

PART 3A IRISH FESTIVALS

1. In pairs/small groups, match the festivals with the traditions below. On which date is each festival?

FESTIVAL	TRADITION	DATE	FESTIVAL	TRADITION	DATE
St. Valentine's Day			April Fools' Day		
St. Patrick's Day			Halloween		
Pancake Tuesday			Christmas Day		
Easter			New Year's Eve		

TRADITION	A. Eat turkey B. Eat chocolate C. Do something romantic D. Play a joke on somebody E. Wear a scary costume F. Eat pancakes G. Sing 'Auld Lang Syne' H. Wear a shamrock

2. Do you celebrate these festivals in your country? What other big festivals do you have in your country?

PART 3B IRISH FESTIVALS - HALLOWEEN

1. Halloween is an ancient Irish festival. Match the modern Halloween traditions to their original meanings below.

HALLOWEEN TRADITION		ORIGINAL MEANING
	*1. People burn big fires in the fields around their town*	To get 'good luck' for having a baby
	2. Jack-O-Lantern - people put a light inside a 'pumpkin head'	So poor people can also celebrate the festival
	3. 'Trick or Treat' - people go to other people's houses and ask for food or money	To protect your town or village from bad spirits that attack at night
4. 'Bobbing' - try to bite an apple in a bowl of water		So bad spirits don't know who you are
5. Wear a mask		To help you escape from the 'spirit world' and come back home

2. Eating *barmbrack* (See picture below) is a typical Irish Halloween tradition. Inside a *barmbrack*, you will find a few surprises. What does each one mean if you get it in your piece of cake?

OBJECT IN CAKE	MEANING
1. A coin	A. You will get married soon
2. A ring	B. You'll have an argument with somebody
3. A stick	C. You will not get married this year
4. A pea	D. You will have money this year

3. Can you think of some traditions for having good or bad luck in your culture?

PART 3C IRISH FESTIVALS – ST. PATRICK'S DAY

Read three "Suprising Facts" about St. Patrick and then look at the questions below.

St. Patrick's Day celebrates everything Irish… but Patrick wasn't born in Ireland.
St. Patrick's colour was blue not green.
The first St. Patrick's Day parade wasn't in Ireland.

ST. PATRICK'S DAY QUIZ – In pairs/small groups, think of possible answers for each of the five questions below.

1. St. Patrick brought Christianity to Ireland. What gods did the Irish believe in before he came?

2. Why did Patrick first come to Ireland? | As a tourist -- As a slave -- For love -- As part of an army |

3. Why do you think 'the shamrock' is the symbol of St. Patrick?

4. Why do you think green became the colour of Ireland and of St. Patrick's Day?

5. The first St. Patrick's Day parade was in Boston in 1737. Who do you think started the parades there?

A. Is there a national day or celebration in your country? Can you make three facts about it and share with the class?

B. What is your country's colour? (The colour your football team plays in etc.) Do you know why this colour is used?

PART 4A IRISH DRINKS

1. Can you match the pictures to the typical Irish drinks and to the occasions Irish people drink them?

1	2	3
4	5	6

DRINK		
i. Cider *ii.* Red Lemonade *iii.* Guinness *iv.* Poitín *v.* Irish Coffee *vi.* Hot Whiskey		

OCCASION
A. Drink a pint of this in the pub
B. This drink is more popular in the summer than the winter
C. Be careful drinking this - it has high alcohol and was illegal in the past
D. You drink this at Christmas
E. Drink this when you're sick with a cold
F. This is popular with children at parties

Picture	Drink	Occasion
1		
2		
3		
4		
5		
6		

2. Have you tried any of the Irish drinks above?
3. What is your country's national drink? When do people usually drink it? Do you like it?

PART 4B THE IRISH PUB

1. Have you ever been to an Irish pub? Are Irish pubs similar to bars in your country?
2. Why do you think Irish people go to the pub? In pairs, look at the box below and choose the things you think Irish people <u>do</u> or <u>don't</u> do in a pub.

IN THE PUB	DO or DON'T	IN THE PUB	DO or DON'T
A. Listen to live music		**F.** Dance	
B. Have a talk with a friend		**G.** Read the paper	
C. Do business		**H.** Watch sport	
D. Go on a first date		**I.** Have lunch	
E. Have a drink with your boss & workmates		**J.** Make plans for your life or career	

THE ROUNDS SYSTEM

3. When a group of three or four people go to the pub, one person will buy the first drink for everybody - *the first round*. A different person will buy the second drink - *the second round* etc.

   Do you think this is a good system? Is there a system similar to this in your country?

ON YOUR OWN

1. Invent a new sport.
2. Ask an Irish person about their favourite Irish sportsperson or team. Report back to the class.
3. Go watch a live Gaelic football, hurling or camogie game. Or go watch some other live sports event in Ireland.
4. Try playing Gaelic football, hurling or camogie yourself!
5. Go to a St. Patrick's Day Parade or go 'trick or treating' at Halloween or go to another typical Irish festival.
6. In groups, invent your own festival. What will you celebrate?
7. Go out as a class and enjoy yourselves. Report back on your Irish 'nightlife' experiences and adventures!

WARM UP

1. What is your favourite film?
2. Have you ever been really scared watching a film?
3. Have you ever cried watching a film?
4. Name one film that makes you laugh.
5. Have you ever watched any Irish films?

PART 1 IRISH FILM - ACTORS

1. Match the Irish Hollywood actors (and the characters they played) with the films and the pictures below.

ACTOR & CHARACTER	FILM	PICTURE
James Nesbitt – 'Bofor'		
Maureen O'Hara – 'Doris Walker'		
Brendan Gleeson – 'Mad Eye Moody'		
Michael Fassbender – 'Magneto'		
Gabriel Byrne – 'D'Artagnan'		
Richard Harris – 'Marcus Aurelius'		
Domhnall Gleeson – 'General Hux'		
Liam Neeson – 'Oskar Schindler'		
Colin Farrell – 'Alexander the Great'		

*A. Schindler's List B. X-Men C. Miracle on 34th Street
D. The Hobbit E. Gladiator F. Alexander
G. The Man in the Iron Mask H. Harry Potter I. Star Wars*

2. Do you know any of the actors/actresses? (You can watch a scene from a film with each actor in the *ONLINE SECTION*.)
3. Who are the most famous actors/actresses in your country?
4. Who is your favourite actor/actress? Why do you like them?
5. In pairs, write some questions to interview your favourite actor/actress.

Co. Wicklow, Ireland

Cillín Chaoimhín
HOLLYWOOD

The Original

PART 2A IRISH FILM GENRES

1. Match the Irish films in the box with the correct genre and description. (Use the film covers to help.)

IRISH FILMS
i. IN THE NAME OF THE FATHER ii. ONCE iii. THE GUARD iv. HIS & HERS v. INTO THE WEST vi. P.S. I LOVE YOU vii. SONG OF THE SEA viii. THE WIND THAT SHAKES THE BARLEY

GENRES	DESCRIPTIONS
1. Musical	**A.** 'A young woman's husband dies. He leaves her ten romantic messages to help her start a new life.'
2. True Story	**B.** 'During the Irish War of Independence, two brothers fight against the British army.'
3. Love Story	**C.** 'A singer plays guitar on Grafton Street in Dublin. He meets a Czech girl. They become friends and sing songs together.'
4. Animation	**D.** 'A real story about a young Irishman and his father who go to prison in England for being terrorists. Both of them are innocent.'
5. War/Historical Drama	**E.** 'Ben and his sister Saoirse (who can change into an animal) travel to the spirit world to help the faeries.'
6. Documentary	**F.** 'Different Irish women, from very young to very old, talk about their relationships with the men in their lives.'
7. Action Comedy	**G.** 'Grandpa Ward gives a horse as a present to his grandchildren. When somebody steals the horse, they travel across Ireland to find it.'
8. Family Adventure	**H.** 'A funny Irish policeman and an American FBI agent try to catch drug traffickers and have some ridiculous adventures.'

Film	Genre	Description
i.		
ii.		
iii.		
iv.		
v.		
vi.		
vii.		
viii.		

2. Have you seen any of the films? You can watch the trailers for the films in the *ONLINE SECTION*.
Which film would you most like to watch?

PART 2B GENRES & DESCRIPTIONS

1. Can you think of an example of a film for each genre below? Which genre of film is your favourite?

1. Science Fiction 2. Romantic Comedy 3. Thriller 4. Western 5. Fantasy 6. Horror 7. War 8. Children's

2. Write a short description for a film you like. Get other students to guess the film, or to say what genre it is.

PART 3A WHAT'S YOUR IMAGE?

1.   Do you have a favourite clothes shop where you buy your clothes? Why do you like it?
2.   How would you describe your own fashion style?
3.   Have you had any bad fashion moments in your past? (Do you have any photos?)
4.   Match the fashion vocabulary to the pictures below. (More than one picture is possible in some cases.)

FASHION VOCABULARY	PICTURES	FASHION VOCABULARY	PICTURES
Jewellery		Alternative Hairstyles	
Hat & Sunglasses		Beards	
Tattoos		Makeup	

5.   Rank the fashion styles in the pictures from '1' (your favourite) to '5' (your least favourite). Say why.

1		2		3		4		5	

6.   Can you think of any other fashion styles that you like or <u>don't</u> like? Find some images online.

PART 3B IRISH FASHION

1.   Is Irish fashion very different from the fashion in your country? How? Which do you prefer?
2.   Look at the styles by Irish fashion designers in the pictures on the right. Which do you like most? Why? *(See the ONLINE SECTION for more information on the designers.)*
3.   In pairs, choose one or two adjectives from the box below to describe each style in the pictures.
     (Use a dictionary to help you.)

> Simple - Casual - Classic - Formal
> Sporty - Elegant - Comfortable
> Individual - Loose - Practical
> Traditional - Young - Cool
> Modern - Old-fashioned - Sexy

4.   TASK: In pairs or small groups, can you design a perfect outfit for a night out in Ireland? You should draw your design and write an explanation of your ideas. The class can vote on the best design and ideas.

PART 3C WHAT COLOUR ARE YOU?

1.   What is your favourite colour to wear? Are the colours Irish people wear different from your country?
2.   Match the colours below with what each says about your personality. (Do you agree with the description for you?)

A. Red B. Grey C. Yellow D. Green E. Blue F. Black	
You are calm, relaxed and loyal	You are mysterious and strong
You are positive and think intelligently	You are passionate and full of energy
You are social, friendly and balanced in your life	You don't want to be the centre of attention

PART 4A CITYSCAPES

1. What is your favourite city in the world? Why? Can you match the famous skylines below to the cities?

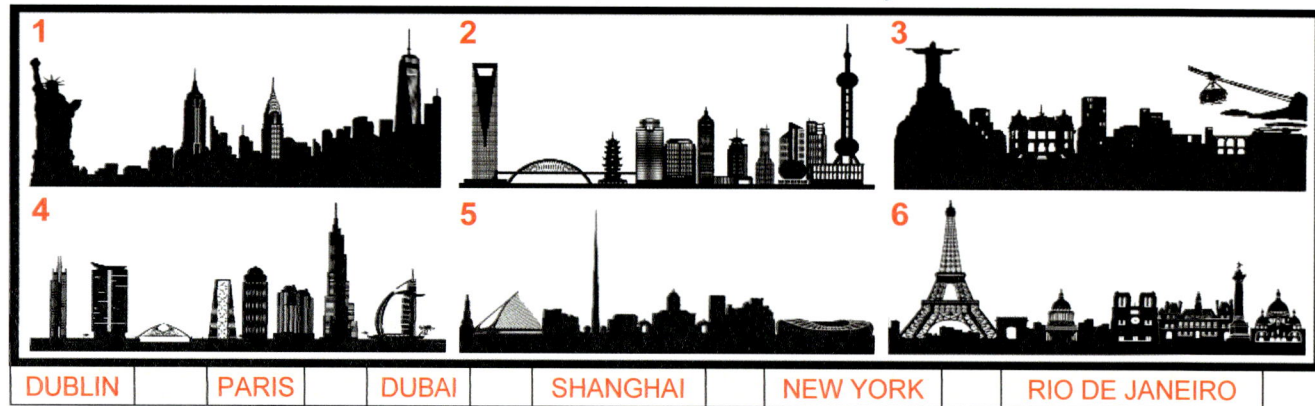

| DUBLIN | PARIS | DUBAI | SHANGHAI | NEW YORK | RIO DE JANEIRO | |

2. Are Irish cities/towns very different from cities/towns in your country? How?
3. **TASK - PART A: Design your perfect city.** Work in pairs/small groups. Think about size, location, climate etc.

PART 4B BUILDINGS

1. What is the most beautiful/ugliest building you know? Can you match the famous buildings below to the country?

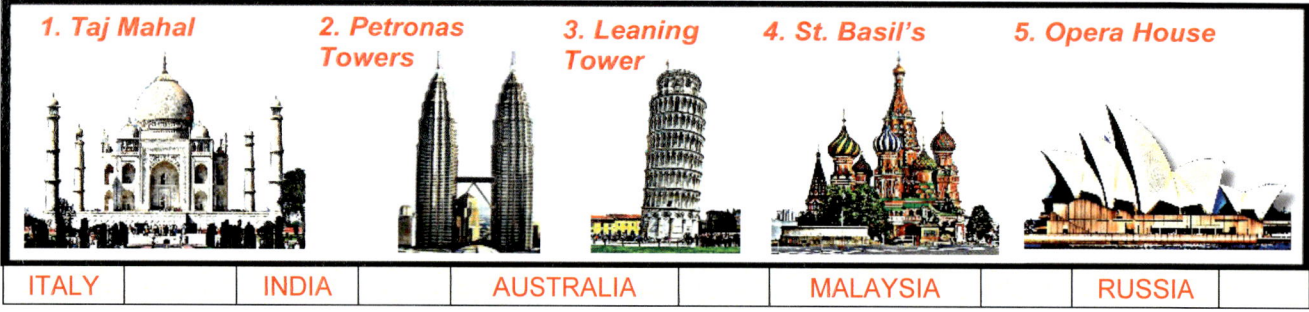

1. Taj Mahal   *2. Petronas Towers*   *3. Leaning Tower*   *4. St. Basil's*   *5. Opera House*

| ITALY | INDIA | AUSTRALIA | MALAYSIA | RUSSIA | |

2. What is the most famous building or monument in your country? Do you know any famous buildings in Ireland?
3. **TASK - PART B: Design a big building or monument for your perfect city.**

PART 4C YOUR DREAM HOME

1. Look up the meaning of the words. Point out the features on the houses in the pictures. *Slanted roof - flat roof - chimney - floods - shade - posts.*
2. Match the descriptions and pictures to the countries in the grid below.

| **A. Cold snowy weather.** South-facing windows to get lots of sun. A slanted roof so the snow falls off. A chimney for fires. |
| **B. Lots of rain & dark winters.** A slanted roof so the rain falls off. A chimney for fires. Large windows to get lots of light. |
| **C. Hot, humid & rainy.** Built on high posts to protect from insects, animals and floods. A slanted roof. Open windows to let cool air in. |
| **D. Very hot & sunny. Very little rain.** A flat roof. Thick walls so it's cool inside. Small windows and balconies with shade from the sun. |

COUNTRY	THAILAND	EGYPT	SWEDEN	IRELAND
DESCRIPTION				
PICTURE				

3. **TASK - PART C: Can you design your perfect house to live in your invented city?**

ON YOUR OWN

1. Listen to different types of instrumental music. Close your eyes and imagine a scene for a new film. Open your eyes. Write the scene. Make your own short films and have an Oscar night with prizes for Best Film/Best Actor etc.
2. Walk around an Irish city/town. Look at the buildings and how people dress. Make notes and report back.

UNIT 12 IRISH SCIENCE & LOVE

WARM UP

1. What thing in your life could you <u>not</u> live without?
2. We normally use a clothes hanger to hang clothes. What other things could you use a clothes hanger for? *(Eg. A TV antennae.)*

PART 1A TEN WORLD INVENTIONS

1. Match the inventions with When/Where each was invented?

1 Velcro	2 Cinema	3 Lego
4 Flushing Toilet	5 Coffee	6 Paper
7 Car	8 Glasses	
9 Internet	10 Zero	

WHEN/WHERE
2nd C. China
7th C. India
10th C. Ethiopia
1280 Italy
1596 UK
1886 Germany
1890s France
1948 Switzerland
1958 Denmark
1969 USA

2. Which inventions above do you think are the most useful?

In pairs/small groups, can you think of…

1. … three other very important inventions in history.
2. … three useful modern inventions you use everyday.
3. … one bad invention you would like to <u>un</u>-invent.
4. … one new invention that the world really needs.

Top 3 Inventions in History	Top 3 Modern Inventions
Bad Invention	New Invention

Compare your answers with other groups.

Which is your favourite quote? Why?

"Necessity is the mother of invention."
– Aristotle
"People will never make an invention more beautiful than nature."
– Leonardo da Vinci
"Inventors should ignore the rules."
– Helen Frankenthaler
"To be an inventor you need a good imagination, time & lots of things."
– Thomas A. Edison
"Inventions are made by lazy people looking for easier ways to do things."
– Robert A. Heinlein
"Only two things are forever – the universe & human stupidity but I'm not sure about the first one."
– Albert Einstein
"If it's green, it's biology.
If it smells bad, it's chemistry.
If it doesn't work, it's physics."
– Guide to Science
"There are no strangers here, only friends you haven't yet met." – WB Yeats
"When you're Irish, you know the world will always break your heart."
– Virginia Henley
"The best way to stop being in love is to get married." – Irish Proverb

What do you think about the quotes? Can you think of any similar quotes from your culture?

"How interesting! A new scientific report says that 50% of people think scientific reports are boring."

PART 1B TEN IRISH INVENTIONS

i. Match the Irish inventions to the descriptions below and to the timeline of when each was invented.

| 1 Ejector Seat | 2 Tank | 3 Rubber-soled shoes | 4 WiFi | 5 Chocolate Milk |
| 6 Tattoo Machine | 7 Heart Defibrillator | 8 Syringe | 9 Football Penalty | 10 Tractor |

DESCRIPTION	PICTURE
A. It changed war forever	
B. It hurts, but then it helps you	
C. An important moment in the game	
D. It's more comfortable to walk	
E. It can save your life	
F. Children like this	
G. It changed farming forever	
H. It can make you look cool	
I. You can stay connected	
J. You can make a quick escape	

TIMELINE		
Which invention is the oldest? *(1680)*		
Which invention is the newest? *(1996)*		
Match 'ejector seat', 'tractor' & 'tank' to the dates		
1911	*1926*	*1946*
Which came first - the *defibrillator* or the *syringe?*		
(1844)		*(1965)*
Which three things were invented in the 1890s?		

2. Choose one of the Irish inventions and find out more about it online. Report back to the class.
3. What are your country's most famous inventions? *(If you don't know any, look them up online.)*

PART 2 GULLIVER'S TRAVELS – SURVIVAL

1. Irish writer **Jonathan Swift** wrote GULLIVER'S TRAVELS in 1726. What do you know about the story? For example, do you know what is special about the island Gulliver visits called **Lilliput?** Look up more information online.
2. After Lilliput, Gulliver travelled to **Brobdingnag**, a land of giants. Everything was twenty times bigger than normal.
   TASK 1: (10 mins) In teams, imagine you are Gulliver. You want to leave Brobdingnag. Before you get in your boat, the giants give you some things to take with you. *(See box below.)* Everything is big, so you can only put six things in your boat. You don't know where you will go. In your team, choose six things to take with you.

Box of matches – handkerchief – biscuit – scissors – map – toothbrush – small mirror shoelace – notebook – key – watch – chewing gum – bottle of perfume – pen – ring – comb

3. After one week at sea in your boat, there is a big storm. Your boat is destroyed. You are now alone on a desert island with only your 6 things. The island is normal sized with lots of trees, plants and water. It is very hot during the day and very cold at night. There are lots of dangerous animals.
   TASK 2: (10 mins) In your team, using only the six things and what you find on the island, you must:

1. Stay cool during the day	2. Stay warm at night
3. Find food	4. Protect yourself from the dangerous animals

4. Present your team's ideas to the whole class. Vote on which team's ideas are best.

UNIT 12 IRISH SCIENCE & LOVE

PART 3A I'D LIKE TO GET TO KNOW

1. Do you like meeting new people? Would you describe youself as sociable or are you more shy?
2. **Close your eyes and imagine...**
   You are walking on a beach. The sun is shining, there is a soft breeze and you are feeling good. Imagine you see someone on the beach who you would really like to meet or to know better. Go sit beside this person and talk to them for as long as you want. Notice all the good sensations you experience. When you're ready, say goodbye to the person. Come back to the class. Slowly open your eyes.
   Complete the sentences below.

I'D LIKE TO GET TO KNOW...

A person
Who has…
Who feels…
Whose most important possession is…
Who thinks…
And who…
If I want…

If you like, read your sentences to the other students in your class.

PART 3B LOVE - WHAT DO YOU LOOK FOR?

1. Which things below are most important for you in a boyfriend/girlfriend? Put them in order - 1 to 8.

	is patient & kind		is beautiful/handsome
	has a good sense of humour		is from the same culture as you
	is from a good family		has a good job/career
	your family & friends like him/her		is intelligent

2. In pairs, compare your answers. Can you agree on a Top 3?

PART 3C ROMANCE AROUND THE WORLD

1. Is going 'on a date' different in different countires? Match the five countries below to their 'romantic styles'.

	A. IRELAND **B.** SWEDEN **C.** FRANCE **D.** KOREA **E.** ARGENTINA
	We like to eat good food and drink wine. We talk seriously about love and romance
	We are passionate in our dance and also in our relationships
	Our relationships are usually quite equal. Men and women are both very independent
	Relationships are usually fun and informal in the beginning here with lots of conversation and joking
	We are polite and also quite traditional. Couples here sometimes wear matching t-shirts and hats

2. Which country's romantic style do you like the most?
3. Are people from your country generally very romantic? Are you romantic?

PART 3D 'WHERE DO I STAND IN THIS RELATIONSHIP?'

1. Describe a typical first date in your country. (Where would you go? Who pays? Etc.)
2. In your country, at what age do people usually get married?
3. In pairs/small groups, can you agree on an order (1-8) for the stages of a relationship?

	To get married		To flirt with someone
	To get engaged		To fancy or like someone
	To go out with someone		To live together
	To go on a date		To meet the parents

4. If you are in a relationship, what were the 'stages' of your relationship? Can you share with the class? Is it similar to other student's experiences in the class?

UNIT 12 IRISH SCIENCE & LOVE

PART 4A 'TÁ MÉ I NGRÁ LEAT'

1. How do you say 'I love you' in your language? Do you know or recognise any of the languages on the right?
2. Which love expressions below are the strongest? In pairs, can you put them in order (1-6) from the least serious to most serious?

I have feelings for you	I like you
I'm in love with you	I'm crazy about you
I'm falling in love with you	I really really like you

3. Look at the love expressions below. Which one do you like most?
   Can you translate any love expressions from your own language?

> Sweetie -- darling -- baby -- my love -- dear -- sugar -- honey

Je t'aime. ti amo. Ich liebe Dich. I love you. te quiero. ik houd van jou. jeg elsker deg. jaG älskar dIG. szeretlek. nakupenda. dji t'veâ vol'ti. amo-te. testimo. maite zaitut. ua here au ia oe. Ech hun dech gaer. mwen enmen. Inhobbok Ahs te obicham. Eg elska thig.

PART 4B THE FIVE LOVE LANGUAGES

i. Can you match the five 'love languages' of relationships in the box with the descriptions below?

1. PHYSICAL TOUCH
2. ACTS OF SERVICE
3. QUALITY TIME
4. RECEIVING GIFTS
5. WORDS OF AFFIRMATION

Giving your boyfriend/girlfriend a present is an important symbol of your love	
Spending lots of time together shows your love	
Doing housework or doing something to help your boyfriend/girlfriend shows your love	
Saying nice things and telling your boyfriend/girlfriend you love them is very important for you	
An embrace, a touch or sitting close together shows your love your boyfriend/girlfriend	

2. Which 'love language' do you think is most important for you? If you are in a relationship, which language do you think is strongest for your own boyfriend/girlfriend? Is it different from yours?

PART 5 FORBIDDEN LOVE

1. Can you think of any reasons why two people who are in love can't be together?
2. Read the story below and answer the questions.

It was a cold, dark night. The two of them were alone together in the house. There was a storm outside with rain and thunder and lighting. She was sitting on the sofa. She felt afraid of the storm. She looked across the room at him sitting on an armchair. She thought he was very handsome. She wanted him to embrace her and protect her from the storm. He looked at her and thought she was very beautiful. There was a big flash of lightning. In that moment, the electricity stopped. She screamed. He ran to the sofa quickly and embraced her. He knew he shouldn't do it... This was a forbidden love. He thought she would tell him to stop but she didn't. She embraced him also. The storm was getting worse outside. Their feelings for each other got stronger. They both wanted to be together. They knew it was wrong and that their families would never understand. Their passion for each other was very strong. They didn't notice the door opening. And they didn't hear the clicking sound of a camera taking a photo...

3. Who do you think the two people are? Why is it a 'forbidden love'? In small groups, think of different possibilities.
4. '...a camera taking a photo…' Who do you think is taking the photograph?
5. Vote on the most probable situation. To see the photo, ask your teacher or check the ONLINE SECTION.

ON YOUR OWN

1. Visit the Science Gallery or Collin's Barracks Science museum in Dublin.
2. Think of somebody important in your life. Send them a message in English to say how much you care about them.
3. An English-speaking boyfriend/girlfriend is great for improving your English. Go find one! Only joking... (Or are we?)

THE IRISH CULTURE BOOK 3
ELEMENTARY/PRE-INTERMEDIATE LEVEL

Why do the Irish drink more tea than anyone else in Europe? How did Irish traditional music help give rock music its rebellious spirit? Do red-haired Irish people really turn into vampires after they die? How does the weather affect how romantic Irish people are? Why are Irish people so happy?

These are just some of the questions that are considered in this book. There are many more.

THE IRISH CULTURE BOOK has three main aims:
- To help you find out about Irish culture
- To help you reflect on your own culture and build cross cultural awareness
- To help you enjoy practising your English

THE IRISH CULTURE BOOK 3 - ELEMENTARY/PRE-INTERMEDIATE consists of twelve units and covers a range of stimulating and thought-provoking topics connected to aspects of Irish culture. The units contain quotes, questions, exercises, authentic reading texts, listenings and links to online resources, as well as problem-solving activities. The discussions allow users to voice their own opinions, to think about Irish culture and by extension their own cultures. The background notes in the TEACHER'S RESOURCE BOOK give clear instructions for every activity as well as extra information and talking points for the discussions, tapescripts and answer keys to the activities. The book can be used by teachers, by students as a self-access book or by anyone with an interest in exploring aspects of Irish culture in a learning or multicultural environment.

THE IRISH CULTURE BOOK provides:
- Opportunities to discuss a variety of topics surrounding Irish culture
- Opportunities to practice speaking skills and fluency
- Motivating questions to engage high-level cognitive skills in English
- A range of interesting quotations on each topic
- Comparative exercises to foster further reflection and thought on other cultures
- Opportunities for follow-up spoken and written presentations
- Adaptable and stand-alone activities that can be used independently or as part of a structured course
- Easy-to-use format with clear explanatory notes and photocopiable materials in the RESOURCE BOOK
- Suggestions and links for a range of follow-on activities and discussions
- An 'On Your Own' section to promote continued learning and project work
- Regularly-updated Online Resources on THE IRISH CULTURE BOOK website

www.irishculturebook.com

Ian O'Malley has worked in ESL - in Ireland, Spain and Italy - since 1996. He has been a teacher, Academic Director and materials designer for language courses. He is an English language examiner and a teacher trainer of ESL teachers. He has an MA in English literature and is a previously published author.

ian@irishculturebook.com